AF395146

SISTERS,

SAINTS

AND

SIBYLS

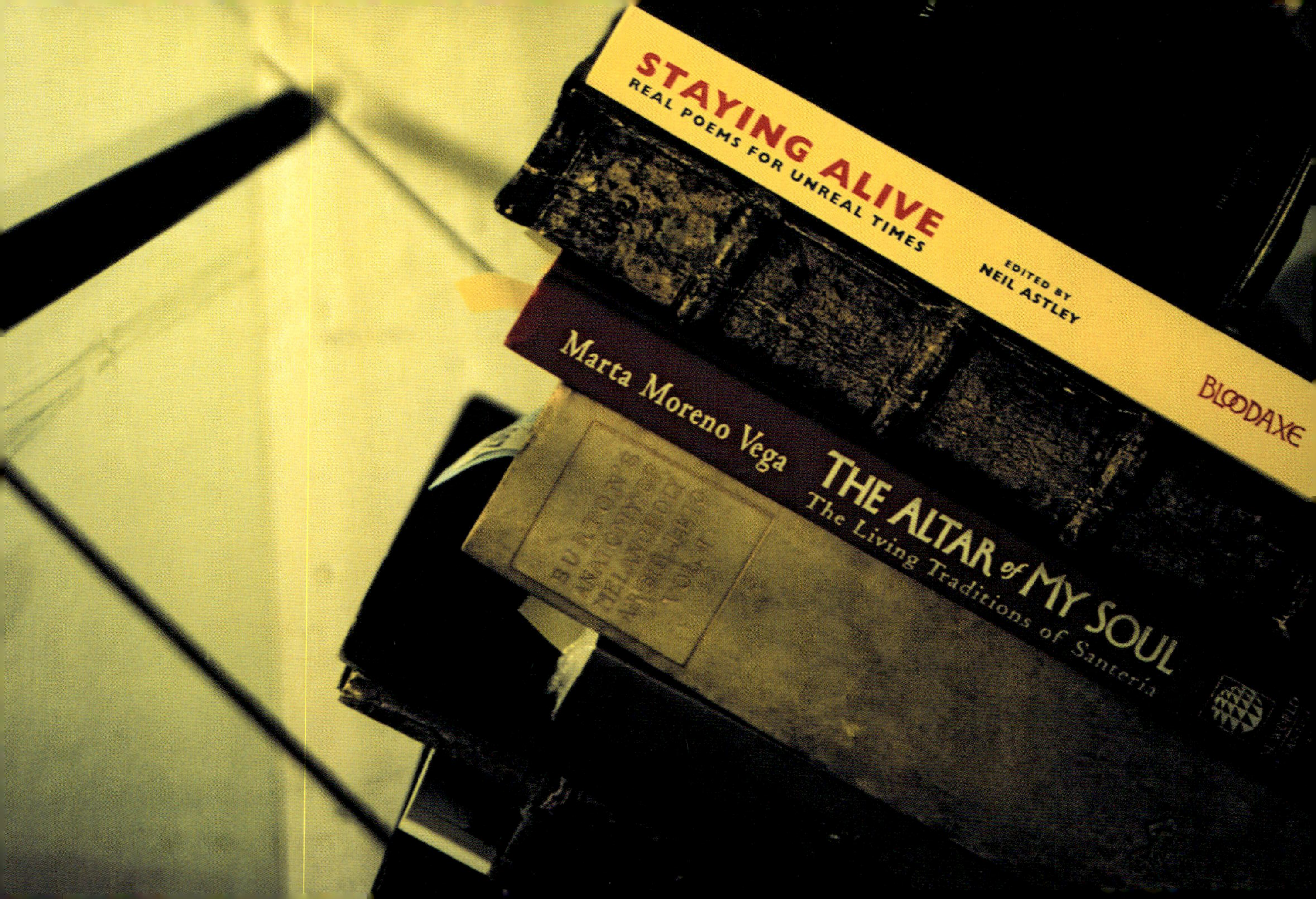
STAYING ALIVE
REAL POEMS FOR UNREAL TIMES
EDITED BY NEIL ASTLEY
BLOODAXE
Marta Moreno Vega
THE ALTAR of MY SOUL
The Living Traditions of Santería
BURTON'S ANATOMY OF MELANCHOLY AB ZWAEBLIU VOL I

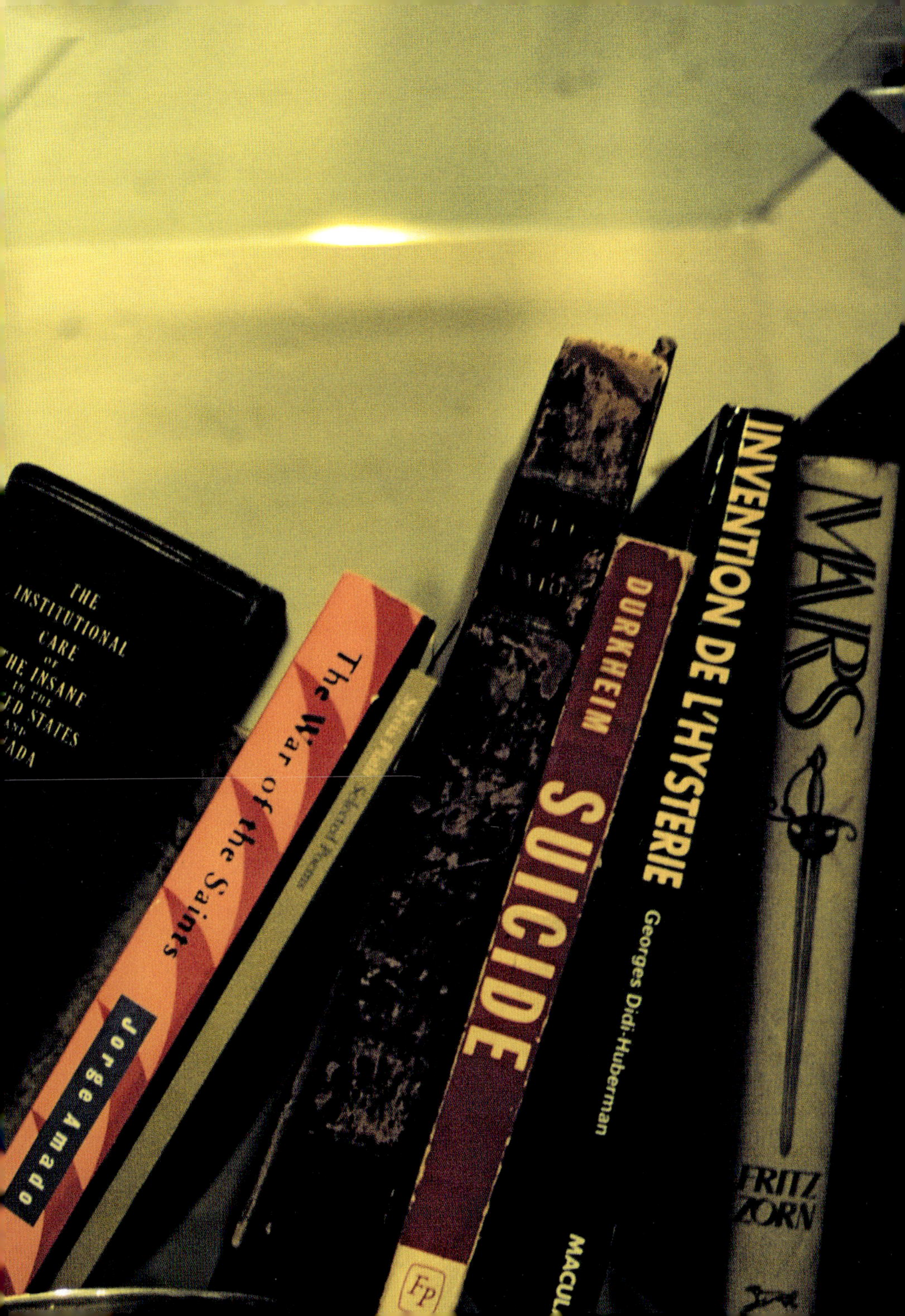
THE INSTITUTIONAL CARE OF THE INSANE IN THE UNITED STATES AND CANADA
Jorge Amado
The War of the Saints
DURKHEIM SUICIDE
FP
INVENTION DE L'HYSTERIE
Georges Didi-Huberman
MARS
FRITZ ZORN
MACUL

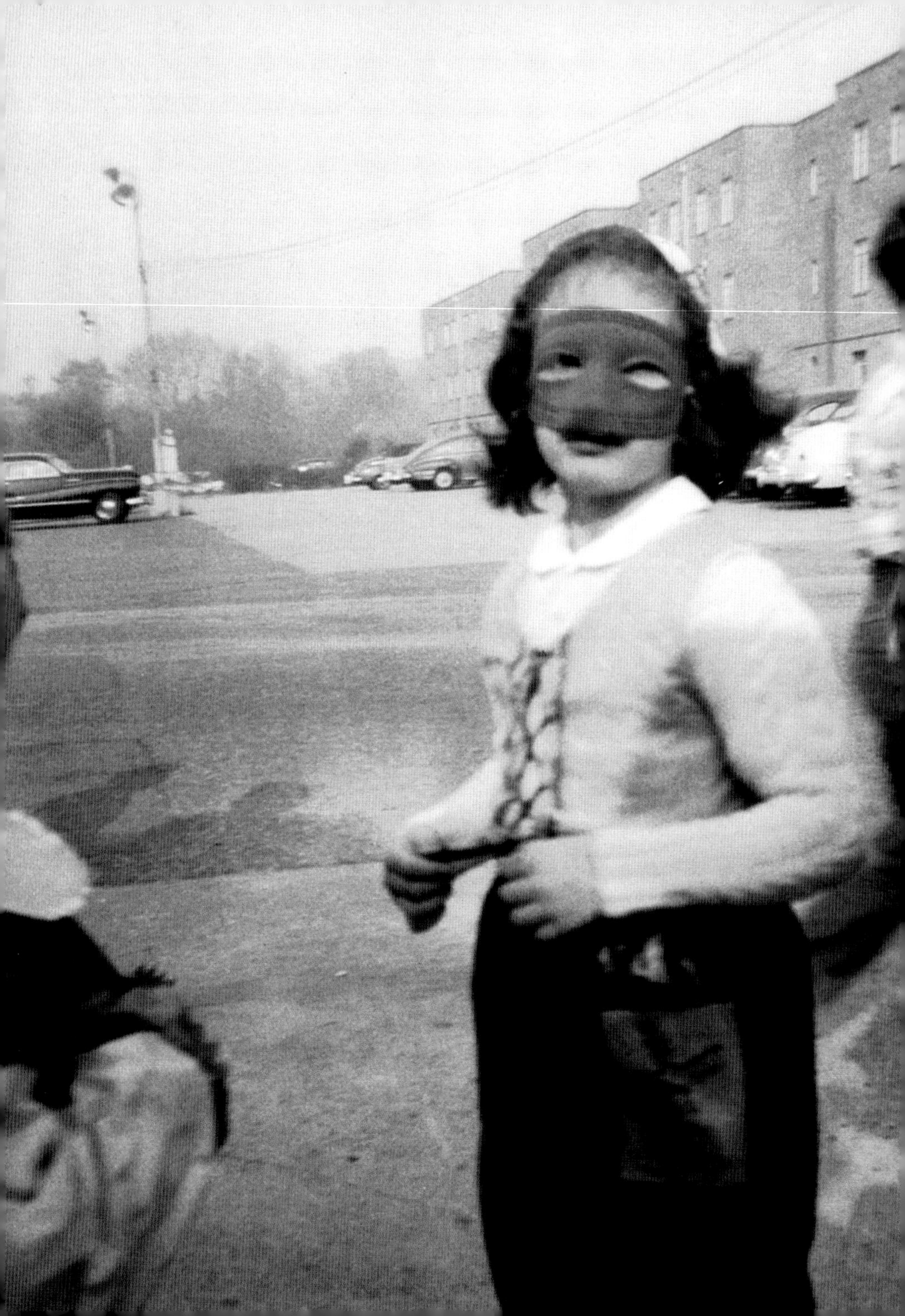

Nan Goldin

Sisters, Saints and Sibyls

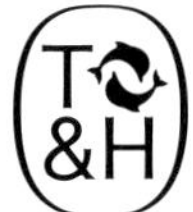

Barbara, who has reached the age of puberty, lives with her father,
Dioscuro. She grows to be a very beautiful girl and is courted far
and wide. Her father is obsessed and decides to build a tower with
two windows to lock her in until she is married. Turning down all
the eligible young men he brings to her, Barbara, lonely and having
no other recourse than introspection, awakens to a spiritual life
and to Christianity. She orders a third window to be built in the
tower as her private symbol of the Holy Trinity, through which
she means to view the world. She baptizes herself with water which
trickles miraculously from the walls of her prison. She tells her
father that she will now devote her life to God. Flying into a
rage, Dioscuro attempts to stab her with his sword, but she escapes.
Betrayed by a shepherd, she is then captured. Though tortured,
humiliated, flogged and mutilated, Barbara refuses to betray her
faith. She is sentenced to death and her father says he will behead
her himself. After commiting this act he is instantly struck by
a lightning bolt and reduced to a small heap of ashes.

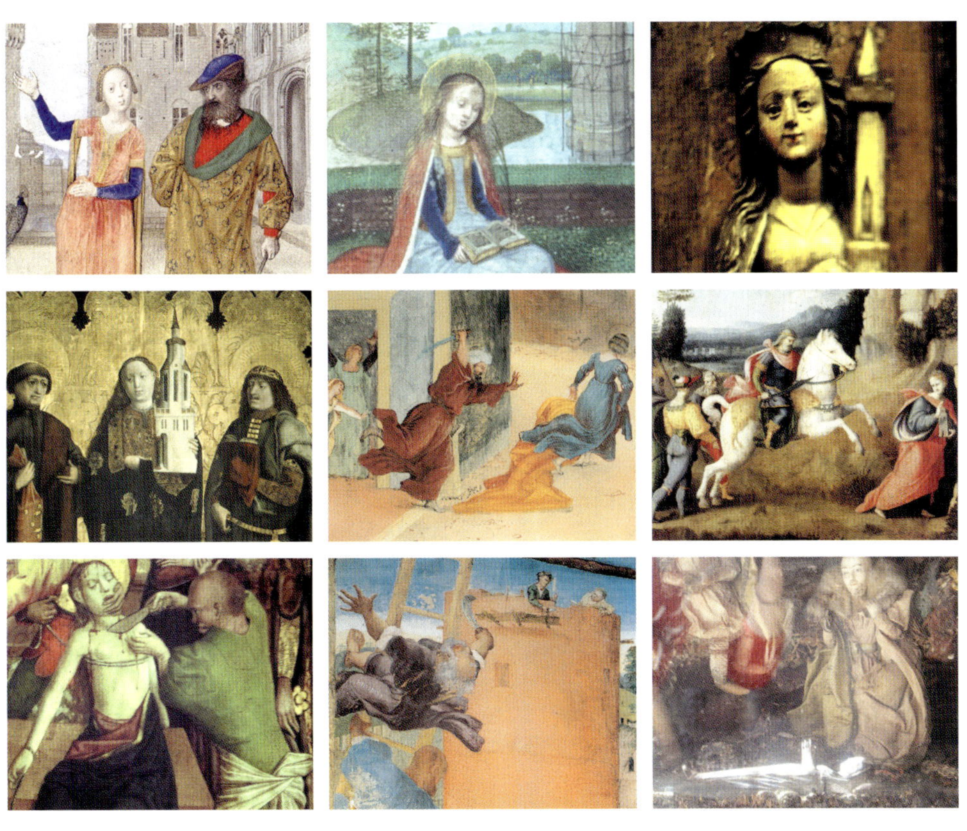

The story of Saint Barbara, date of birth December 4, 253, Nicomedia, Turkey

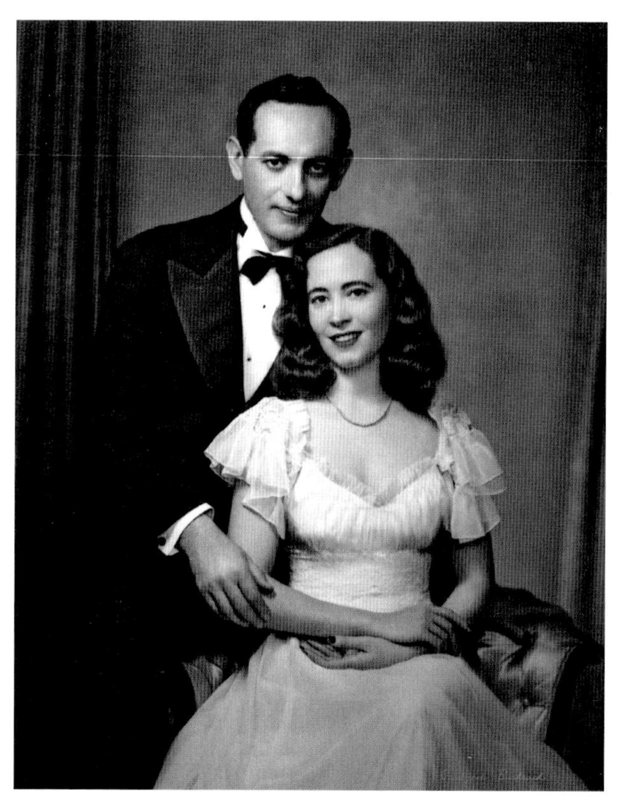

MY PARENTS WERE MARRIED
ON SEPTEMBER 3, 1939, THE
SAME DAY WAR WAS DECLARED.

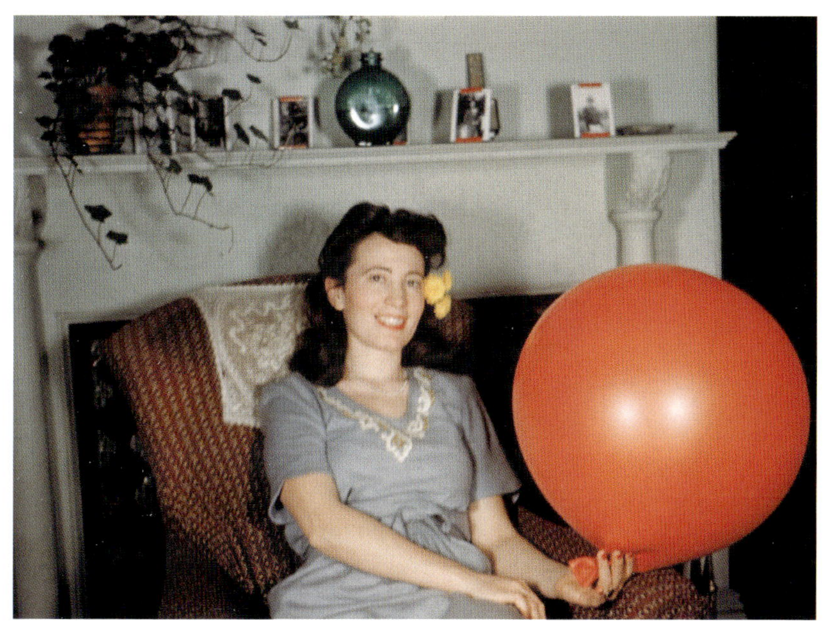

My father wanted
his first child to be a boy.

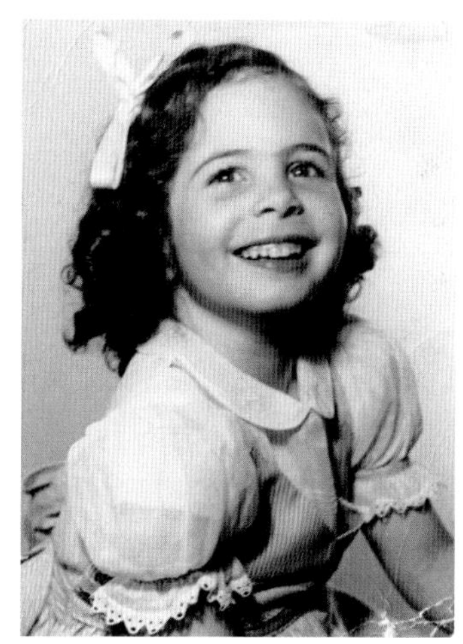

"BARBARA HOLLY GOLDIN.
BORN 21 MAY 1946. SEX: FEMALE."

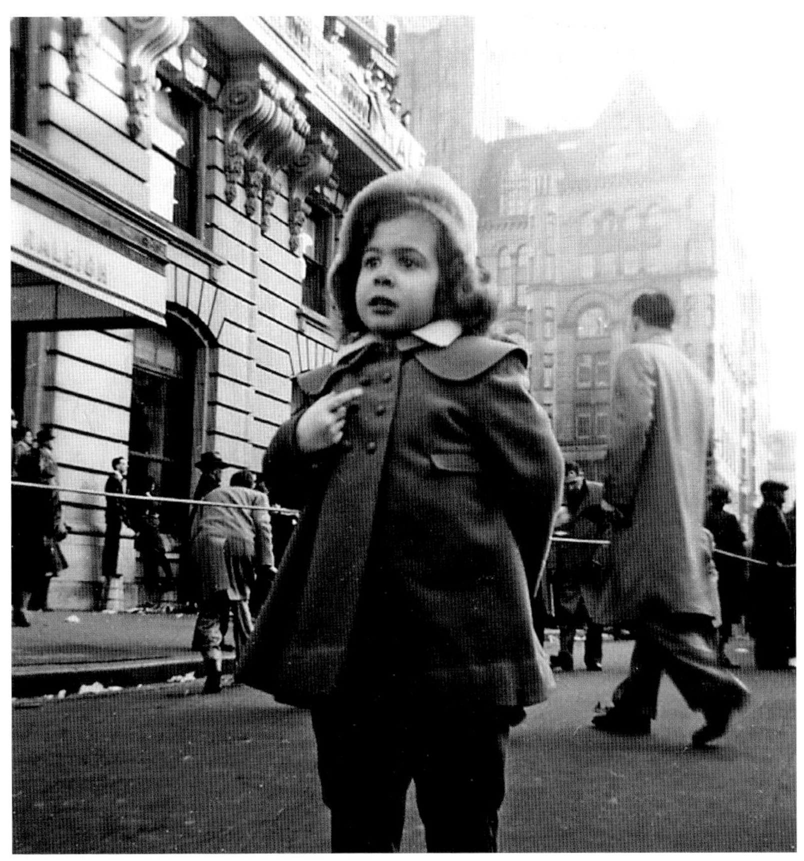

BARBARA IN THE CITY AT 15 MONTHS, WASHINGTON, D.C., 1947

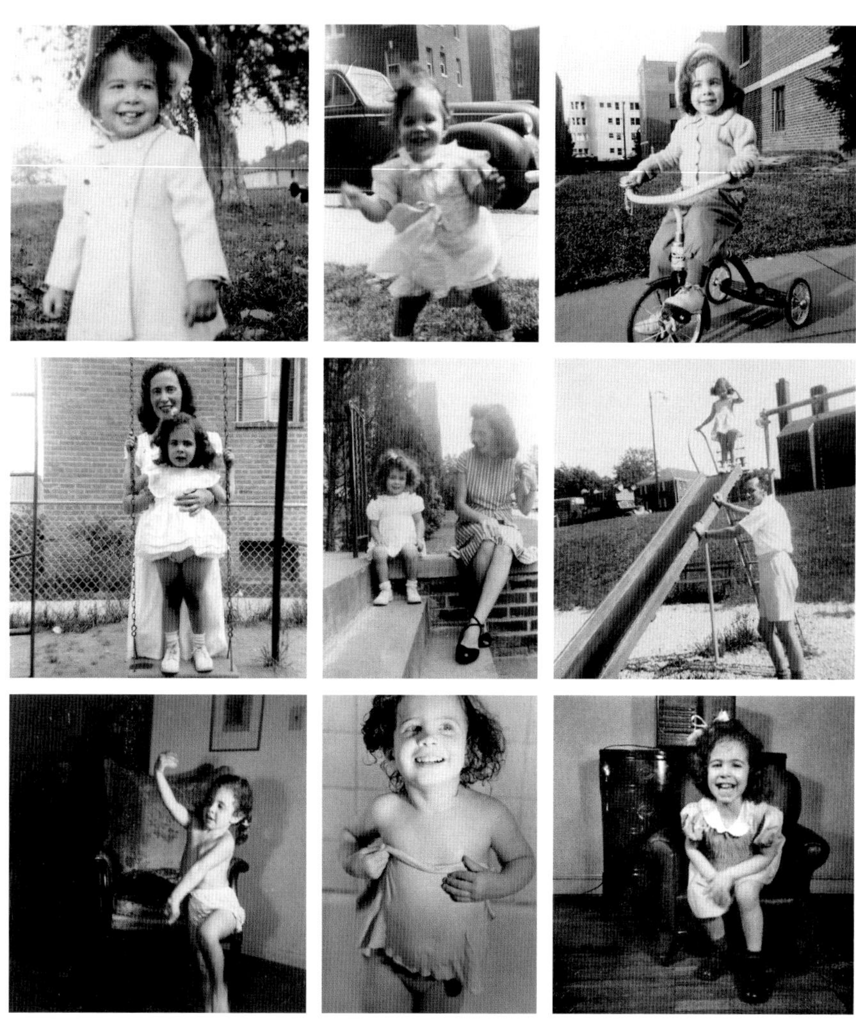

Barbara, up to 2 years old, in The Projects, Washington, D.C., 1946–1948

"Barbara was a precocious child who
walked at seven months and could talk
at about a year's age. Because her mother
insisted on her speaking in perfect sentences,
which she could not perform,
she stopped speaking altogether when
she was about one and a half years old.

When Barbara was 2 years old,
her mother was referred to a psychologist
for help in handling the child."

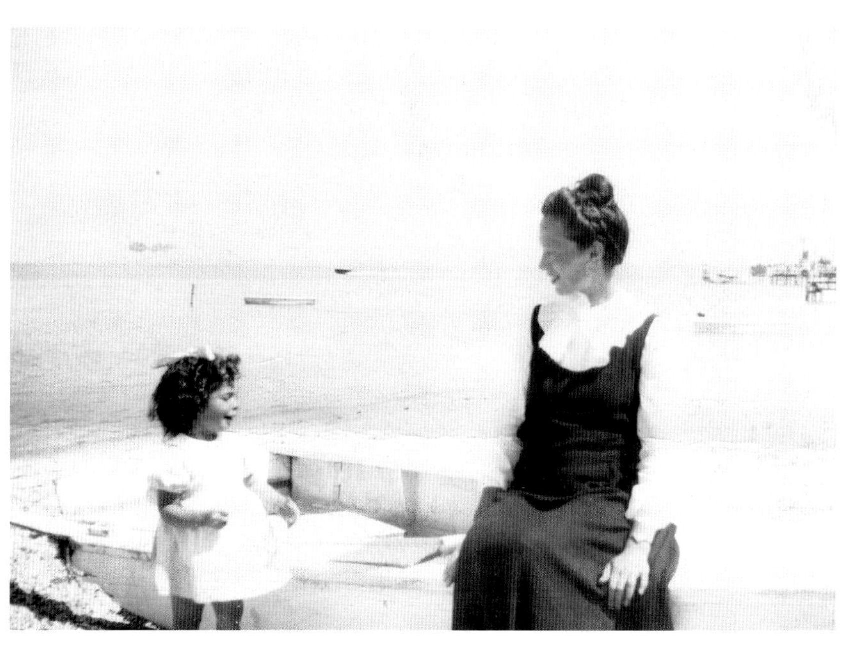

BARBARA ALMOST 2 WITH LIL PREGNANT, 1947

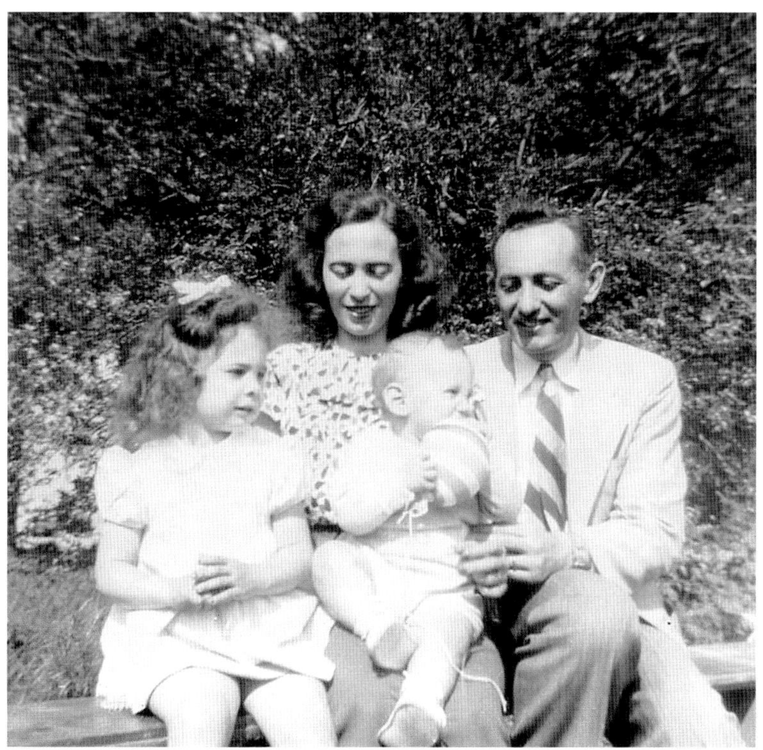

My oldest brother was born
on my father's birthday. He quickly became
the focus of my father's full attention.

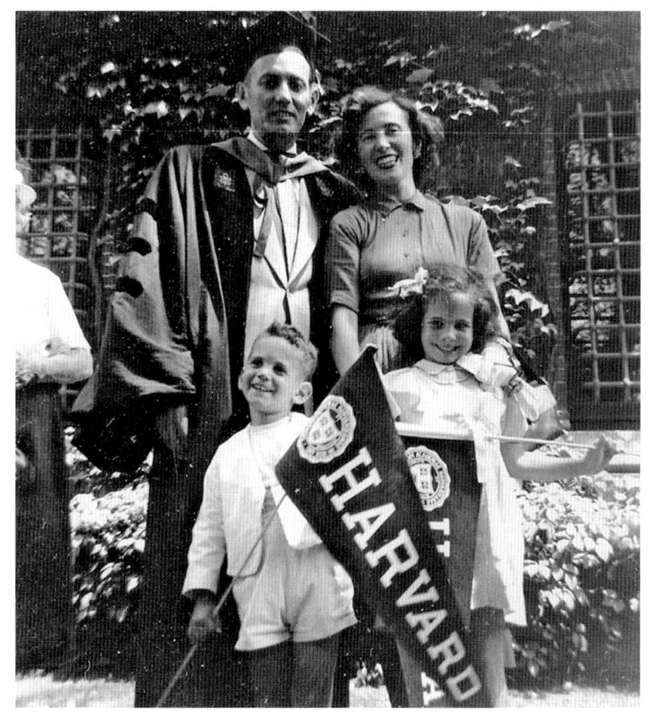

Harvard reunion, Cambridge, Massachusetts, 1951

"Barbara began school. She was
sparkling, bright, neat, and well
cared for. She shined at school;
that was expected of course."

"Harvard" was the fisrt word we learned.

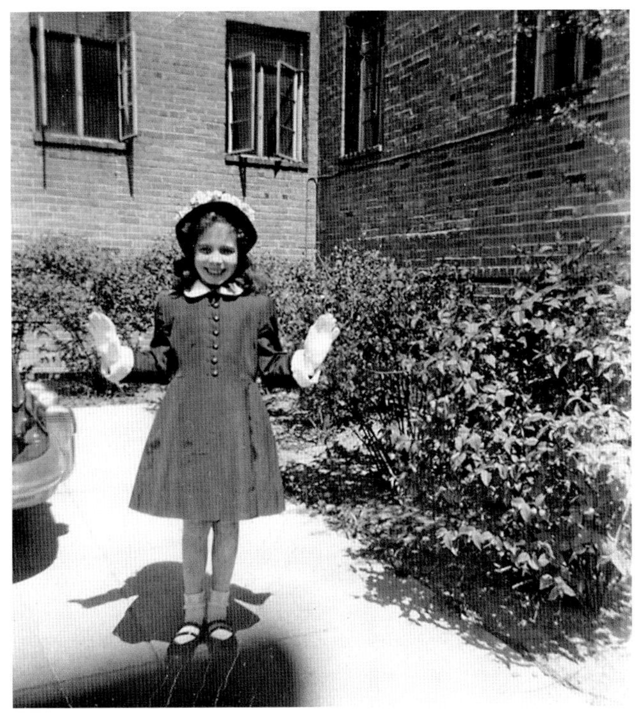

BARBARA IN THE COURTYARD, THE PROJECTS, WASHINGTON, D.C., 1952

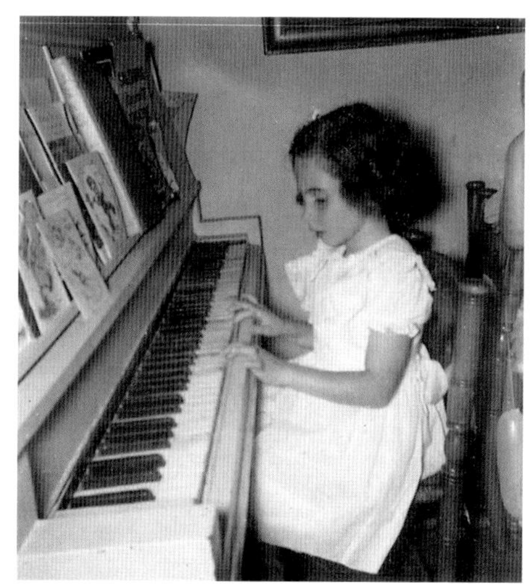

BARBARA PLAYING THE PIANO AT HOME, 1951

"BARBARA, WHO HAD
STARTED PLAYING THE PIANO
AT THE AGE OF 4, BEGAN
TAKING LESSONS FROM THE
AGE OF 6."

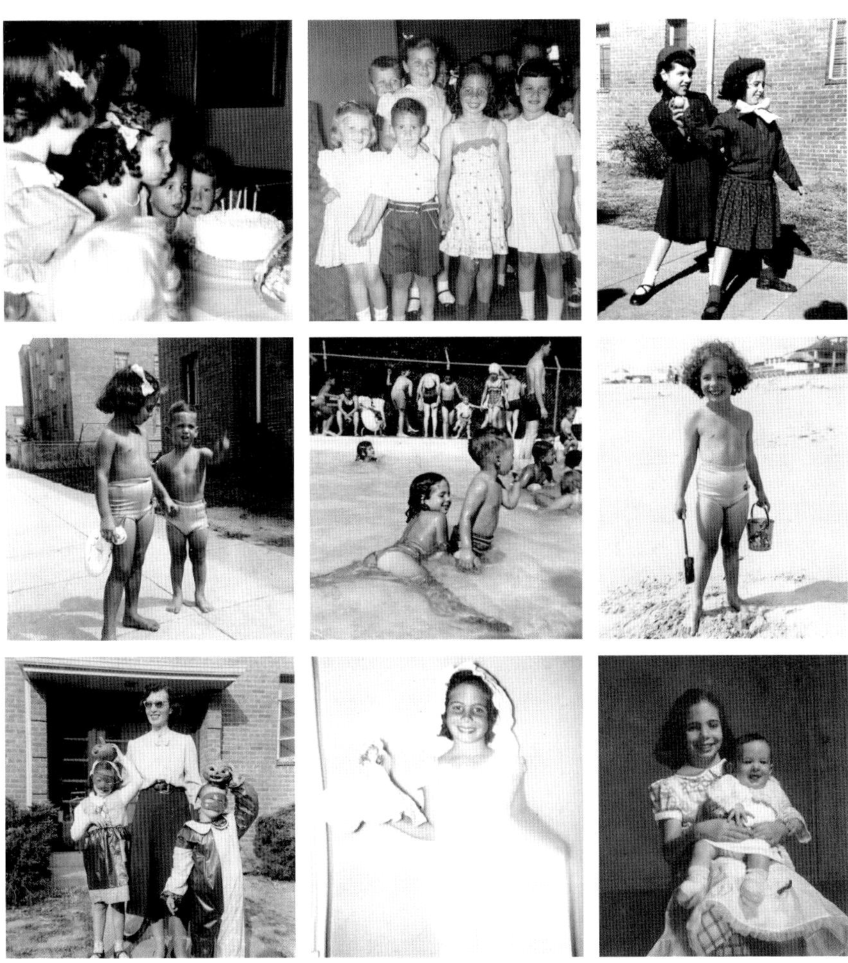

Barbara age 5 to 7 years, Washington, D.C., 1951-1953

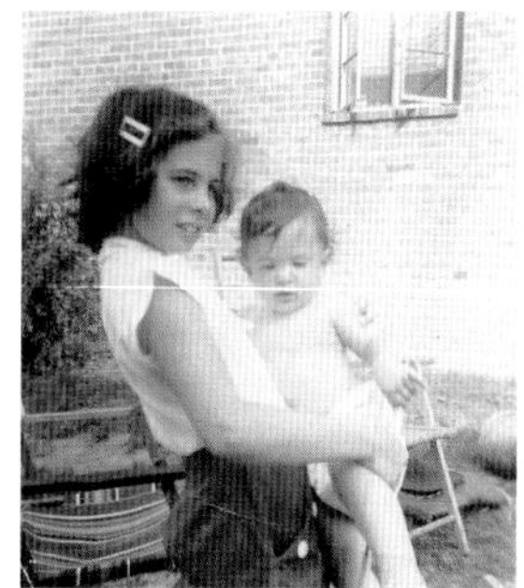
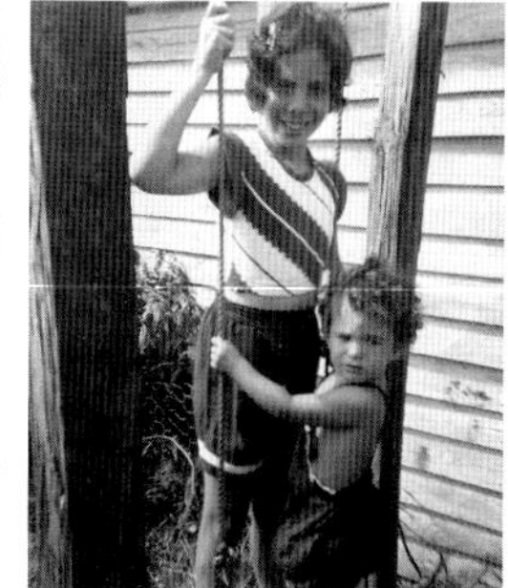
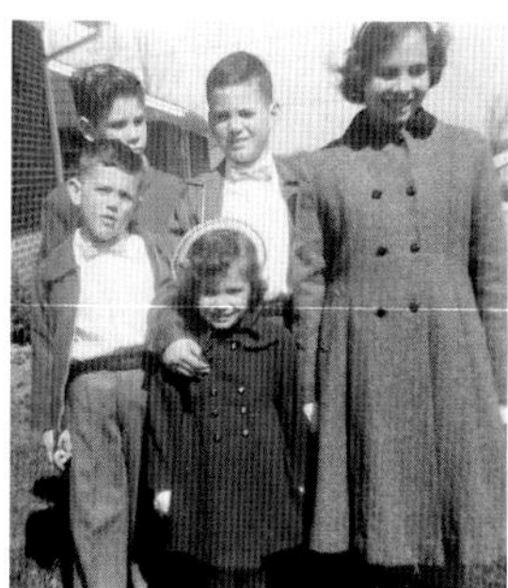

Barbara with Nan age 8 to 12 years, 1954-1958

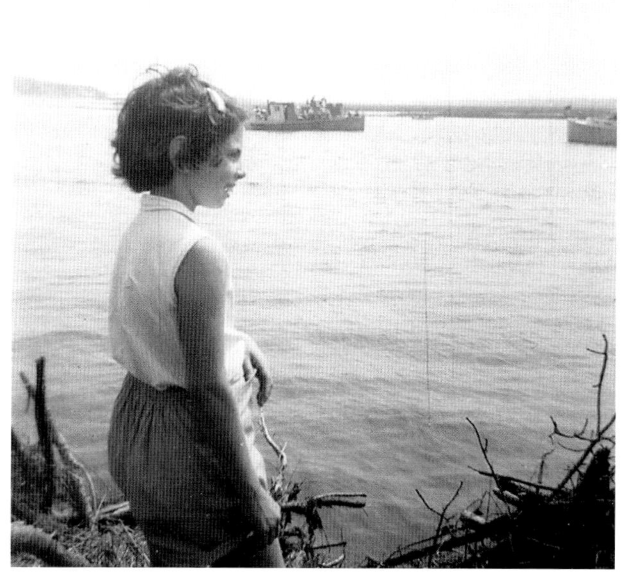

Barbara, 12 years, 1958

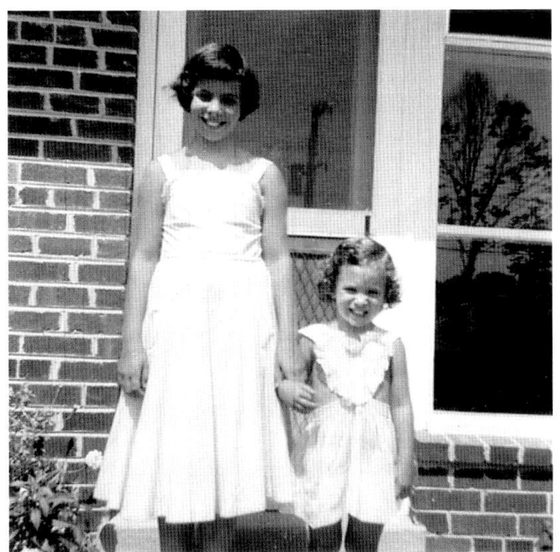

BARBARA 11 YEARS, NAN 4 YEARS, SILVER SPRING, MARYLAND, 1957

MY SISTER TAUGHT ME TO WATCH THE
SUNSET. SHE WASHED MY HAIR. SHE USED
TO PLAY MOONLIGHT SONATA AT
MIDNIGHT, WHEN SHE HAD TO BABYSIT
FOR ME. SHE LIKED TO MOTHER ME.
I WAS HER CONFIDANTE.

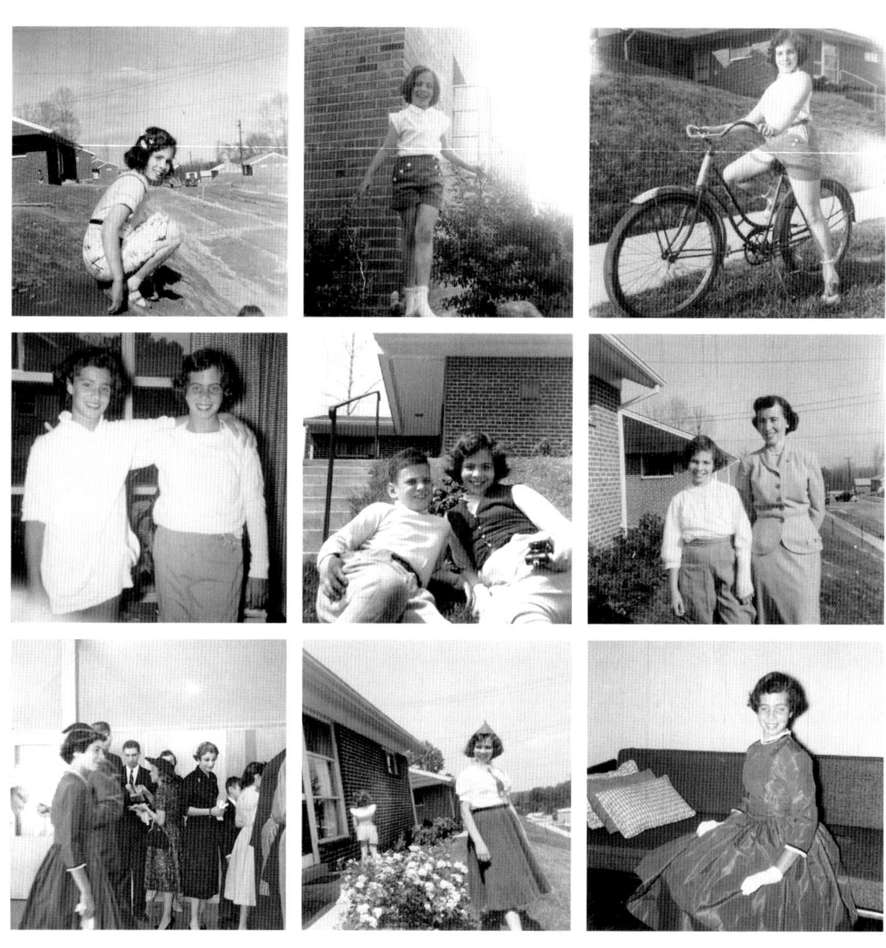

Barbara age 11 to 12 years, Silver Spring, Maryland, 1957-1958

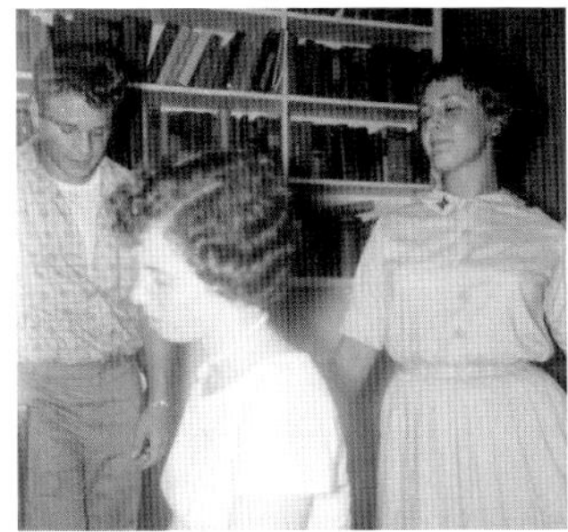 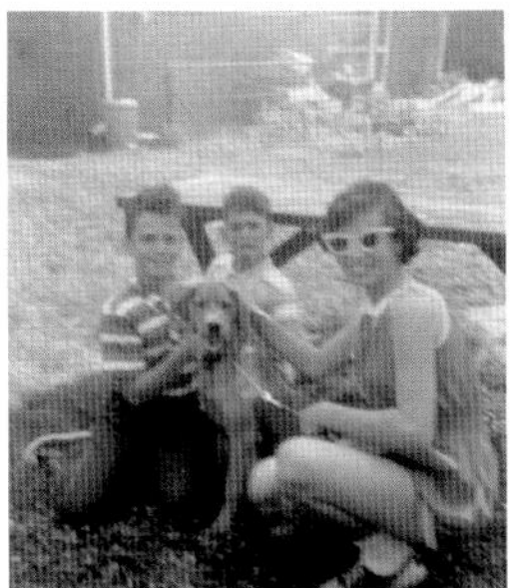 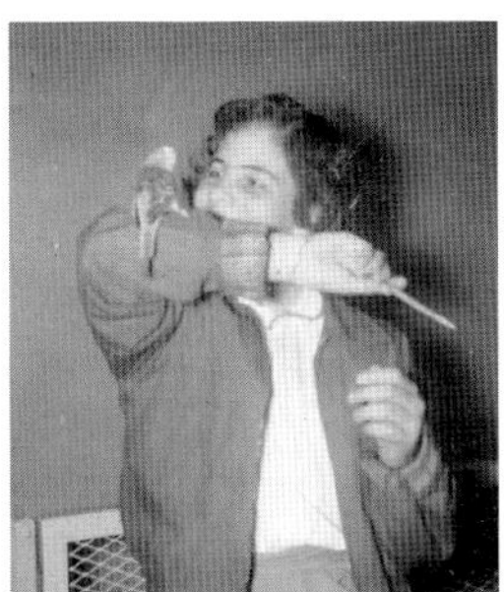

Barbara, age 12 to 13, 1958–1959

"The troubles started between the mother and Barbara when she was about 12. They were always fighting and there was a lot of violence in the house. The father stayed silent on the side."

I grew up to constant screaming and objects being thrown. The dinner table was a battle ground.

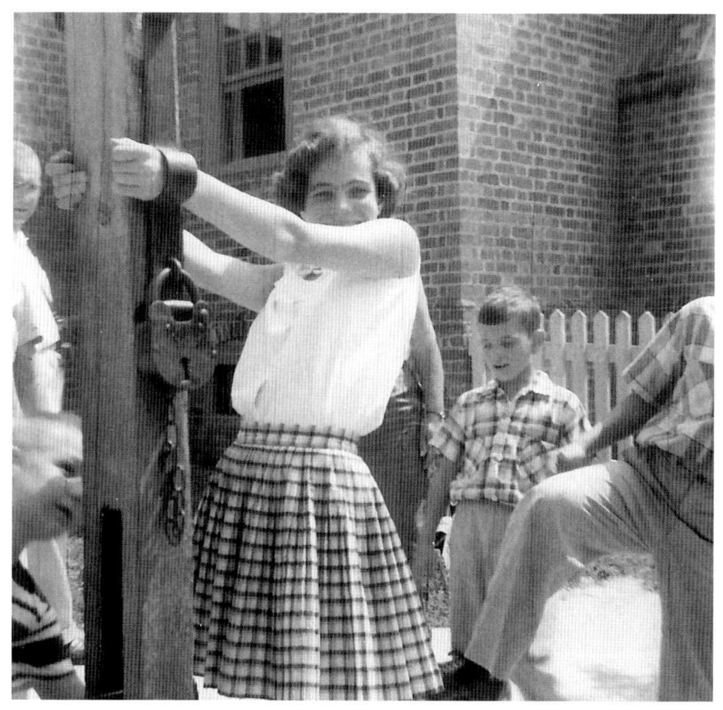

Barbara during a family vacation, Salem, Massachusetts, 1959

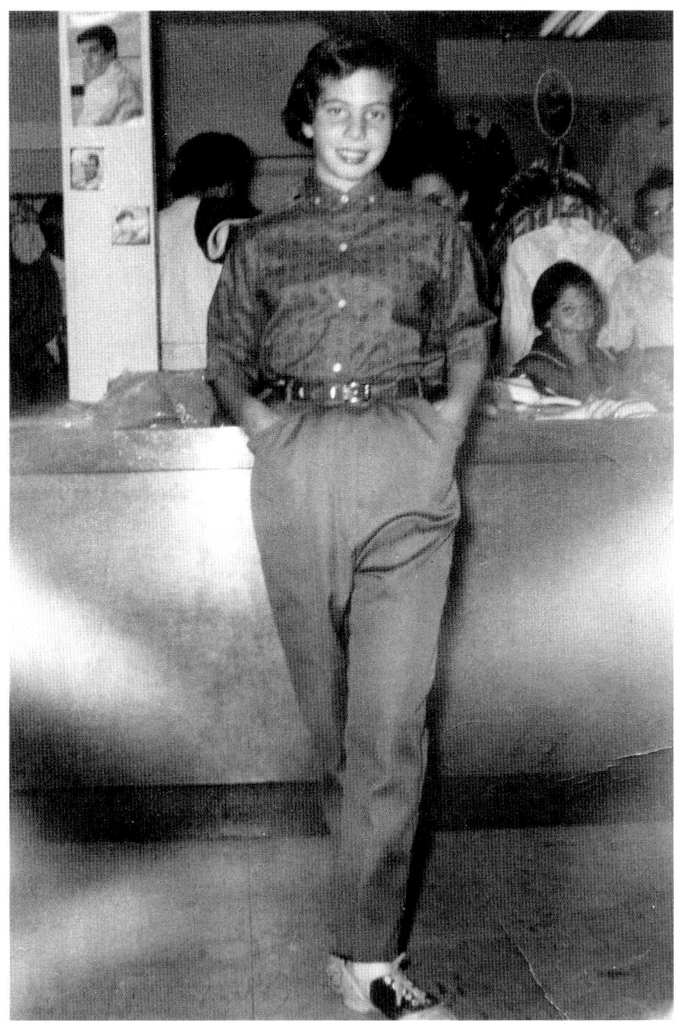

Barbara modeling at 14, 1960

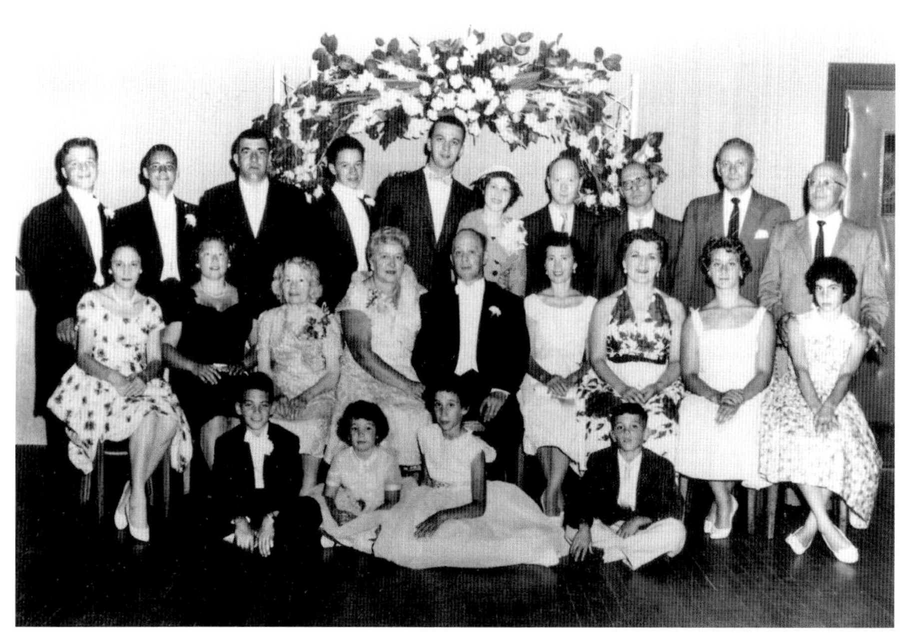

WEDDING OF OUR COUSINS, BOSTON, MASSACHUSETTS, JUNE 1959

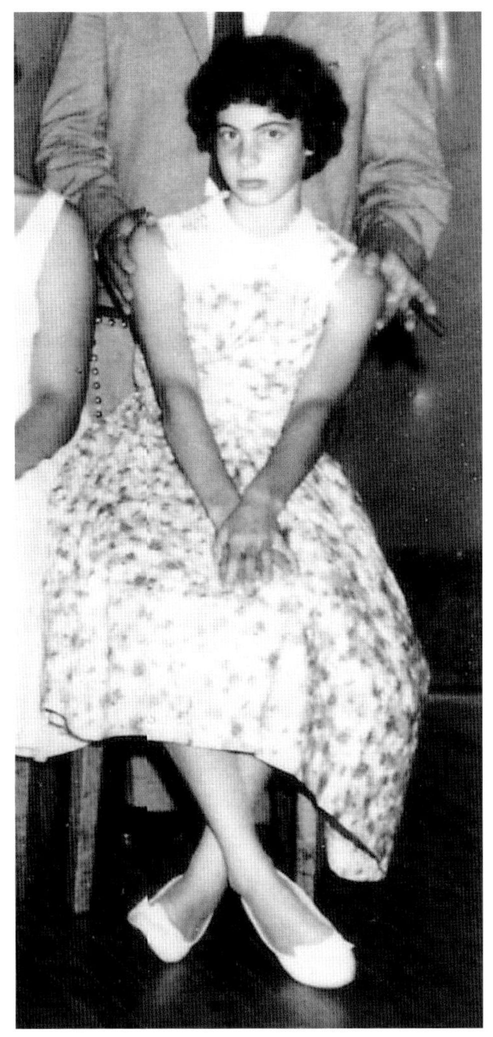

BARBARA AT THE WEDDING, AGE 13, JUNE 1959

My sister started to go to the movie theater
on Saturday afternoons to make out with
unknown, "undesirable" and older boys.
My parents were very frightened, "pregnancy
out of marriage was the greatest sin possible."
My parents, on the advice of a psychiatrist,
sent her to a detention center 300 miles
away from home.

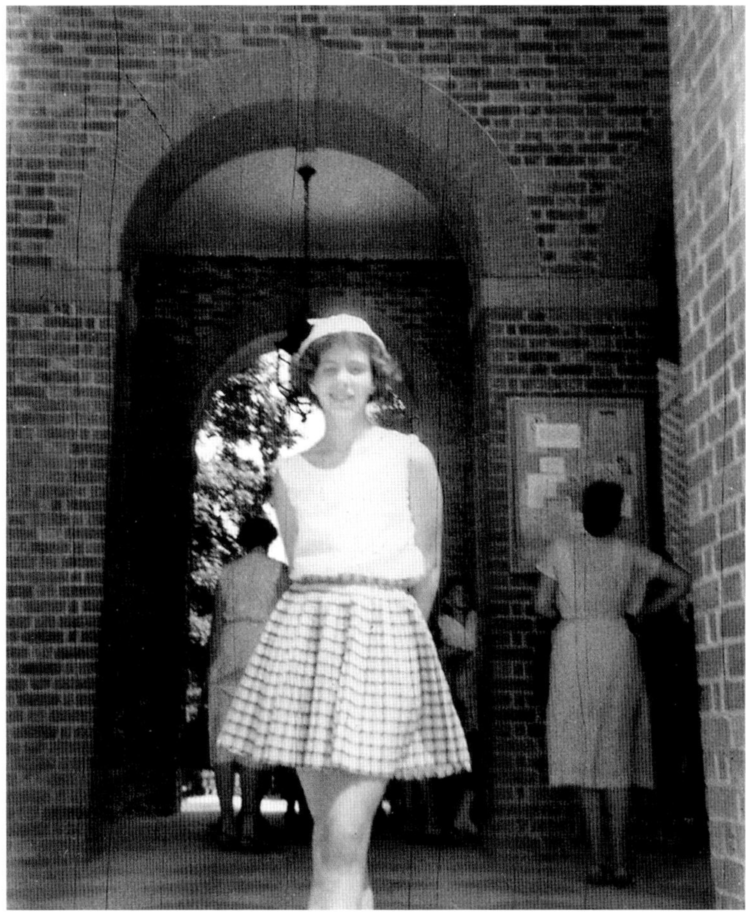

Barbara, age 14, 1960

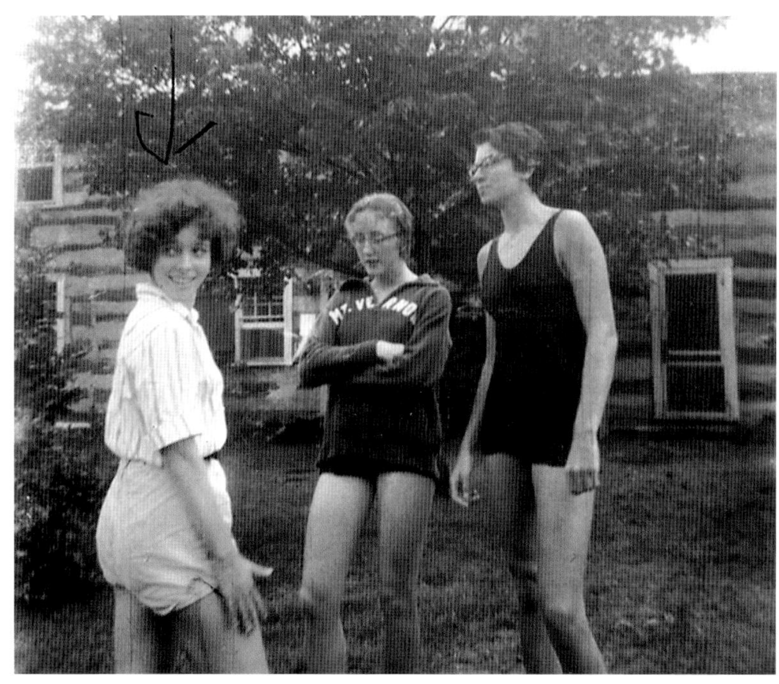

Barbara with friends, Bellefaire School for Wayward Children, Cleveland, Ohio, 1960

"Name: Barbara Goldin.

Age at intake: 14.

Reason for referral: The onset of acting-out behavior occurred when she was aged twelve, open defiance, physical abuse of the mother, sexually provocative behavior, and association with 'undesirable friends.' She became 'loud and coarse in speech,' and threatened to become a prostitute."

Next page: Register of orphans, Bellefaire, Cleveland, Ohio, 2004

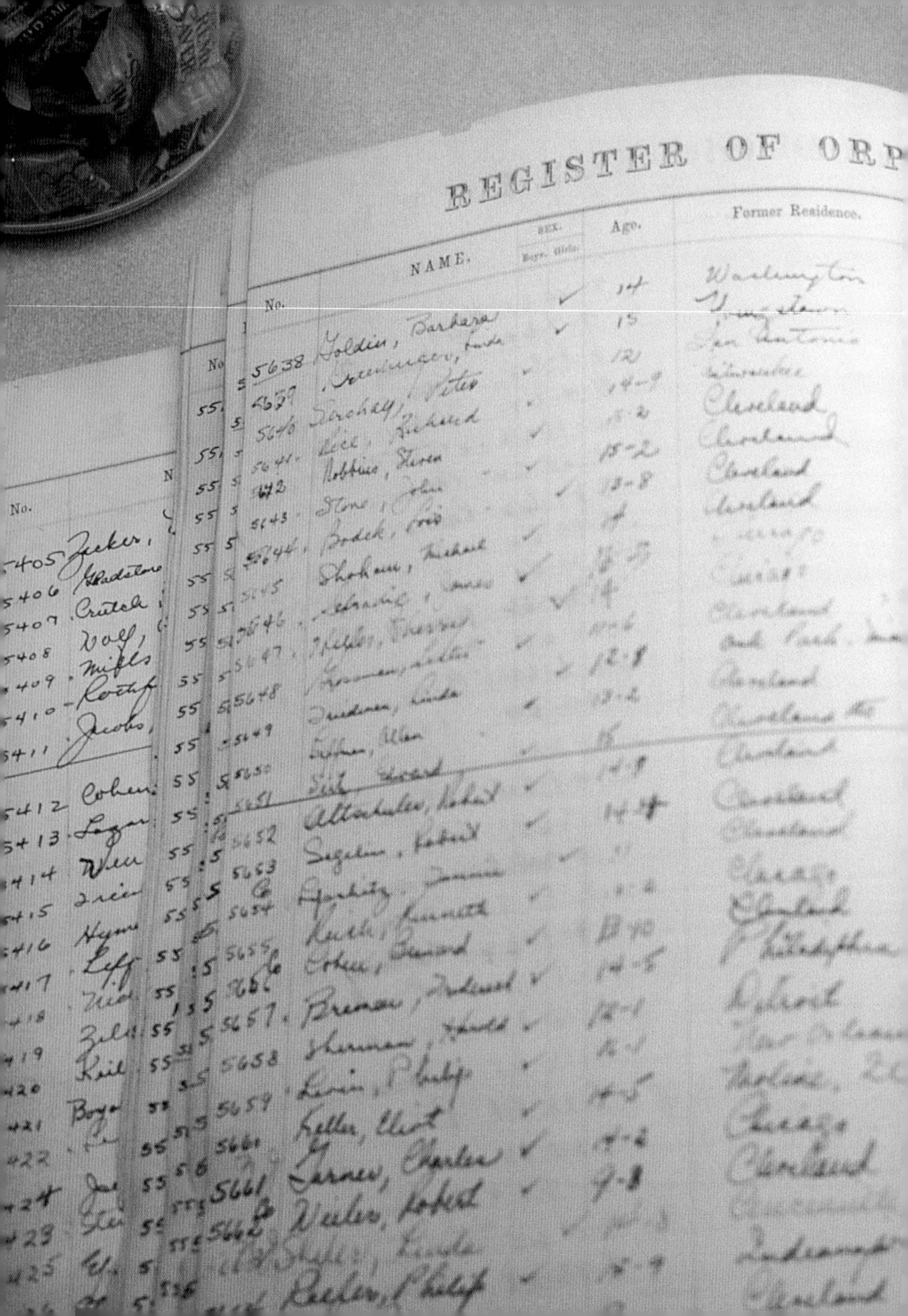

REGISTER OF ORP[HANS]

No.	NAME.	SEX. (Boys / Girls)	Age.	Former Residence.
		✓	14	Washington
		✓	15	[Youngstown]
5638	Goldin, Barbara		12	San Antonio
5639	[Seemann], Linda		14-9	Milwaukee
5640	Sirchaly, Peter		15-2	Cleveland
5641	Nice, Richard		15-2	Cleveland
5642	Nobbins, Steven		13-8	Cleveland
5643	Stone, John	✓		[illegible]
5644	Bodek, [Fred]			[illegible]
5645	Shoham, Michael	✓		[illegible]
5646	[illegible]	✓	14	Cleveland
5647	Pfefer, [illegible]			Oak Park
5648	[illegible]	✓	12-8	Cleveland
5649	[illegible], Linda	✓	13-2	Cleveland
5650	[Stephen], Allan	✓		Cleveland
5651	Silk, [Edward]	✓	14-8	Cleveland
5652	Altschuler, Robert	✓	14	Cleveland
5653	Segelin, Robert	✓		[illegible]
5654	Gunkitz, [illegible]			Cleveland
5655	Ruth, Kenneth	✓		Philadelphia
5656	Cohen, [Leonard]	✓	14-5	Detroit
5657	Brennan, [Roland]	✓	12-1	New Orleans
5658	Sherman, [Harold]		16-1	[illegible]
5659	Levin, Philip	✓		Chicago
5660	Keller, Eliot		7-2	Cleveland
5661	Garnett, Charles	✓	9-8	[illegible]
5662	Weiler, Robert			Indianapolis
	Skyler, Linda			
	Keeler, Philip	✓		Cleveland

(Left-hand column, partially visible: 5405 Zucker; 5406 Gladstone; 5407 Crutch; 5408 Wolf; 5409 [Mifls]; 5410 [Rochf]; 5411 Jacobs; 5412 Cohen; 5413 [Lazar]; 5414 [Weiss]; 5415 [Price]; 5416 Hyman; 5417 [Left]; 5418 [Nisl]; 5419 [Zell]; 5420 [Kail]; 5421 [Boyd]; 5422 [illegible]; 5424 Jacobs; 5423 [illegible]; 5425 [illegible] — all mostly illegible.)

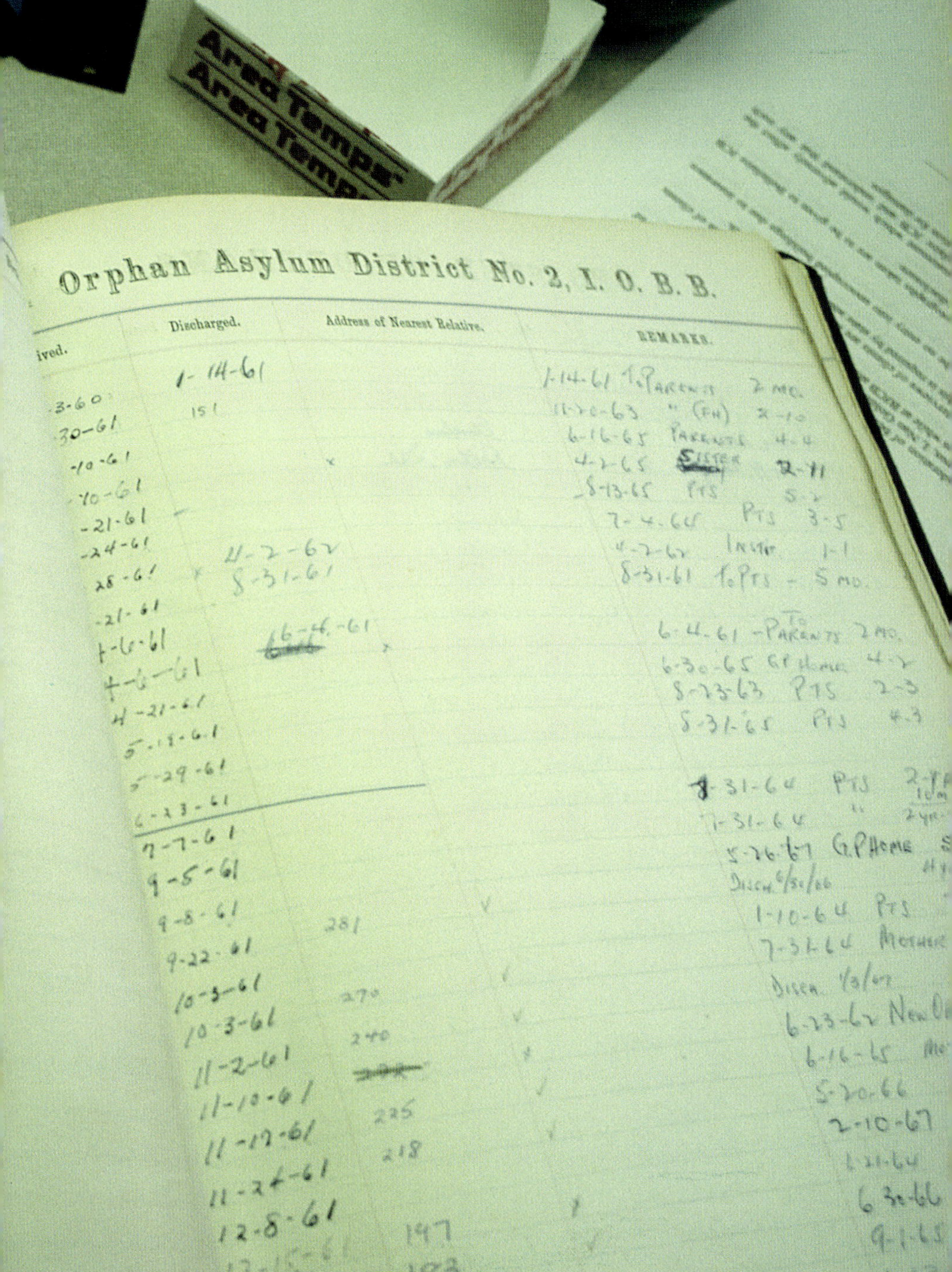

Orphan Asylum District No. 2, I. O. B. B.

ived.	Discharged.	Address of Nearest Relative.	REMARKS.
	1-14-61		1-14-61 To Parents 7 Mo.
-3-60	15t		11-10-63 " (FH) 2-10
-30-61			6-16-65 Parents 4-4
-10-61	x		4-2-65 Sister 2-11
-10-61			-8-13-65 Pts 5-7
-21-61			7-4-65 Pts 3-5
-24-61	11-2-62		4-2-62 Inst 1-1
28-61	x 8-31-61		8-31-61 To Pts - 5 Mo.
-21-61			
7-6-61	16-4-61	x	6-4-61 - To Parents 7 Mo.
7-6-61			6-30-65 Gr Home 4-2
4-21-61			8-23-63 Pts 2-3
5-17-61			8-31-65 Pts 4-3
5-29-61			
6-23-61			8-31-64 Pts 2-10m
7-7-61			7-31-64 " 2yr
9-5-61			5-26-67 G.P Home
9-8-61	281	v	Disch 6/30/66
9-22-61			1-10-64 Pts
10-3-61	270	v	7-31-64 Mother
10-3-61	240	v	Disch 1/2/67
11-2-61		v	6-23-62 New Or
11-10-61	225	v	6-16-65 Mo
11-17-61	218	v	5-20-66
11-24-61			2-10-67
12-8-61	147	v	1-21-64
12-15-61	183		6-30-66
12-29-61			9-1-65

"After one week here, she ran away.
She got as far as Pittsburgh, was returned to
Bellefaire, but almost immediately attempted
to run away again.
She regarded Bellefaire as a mental institution;
sometimes behaving in a way that made
it necessary to put her in a locked room.
She showed self-destructive tendencies
in that she often cut herself on the hands,
face, and legs with a razor.
There was some interference on the part of
the parents, in that they wrote to Bellefaire
giving their idea of Barbara's treatment
and sent Barbara medication,
and razor blades. Her mother followed
that with a letter to the staff wondering
if she should have sent them."

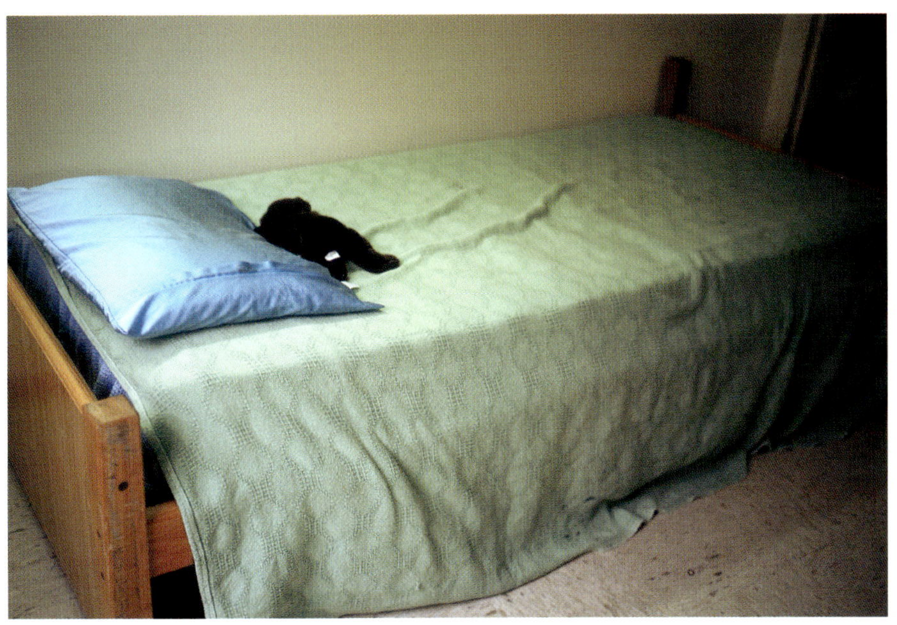

Bellefaire, Cleveland, Ohio, 2004

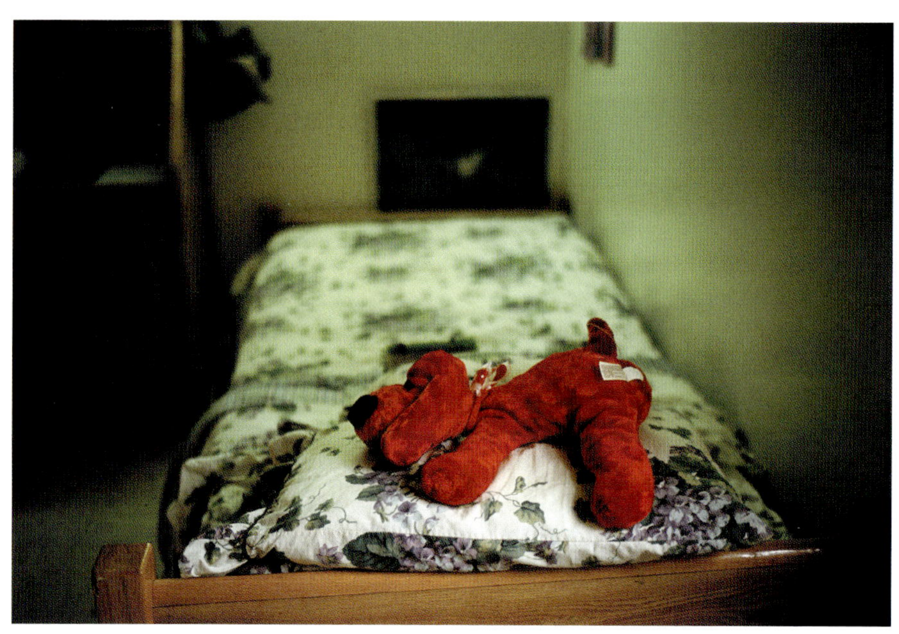

Bellefaire, Cleveland, Ohio, 2004

"Barbara made an attempt to attend school,
did not feel able to remain there, returned
to the cottage, and set fire to her mattress
and curtains, thus necessitating her return
to the locked room and the end of her stay
at Bellefaire."

Age at discharge: 14.

Next page: Bellefaire, Cleveland, Ohio, 2004

April

1 ☆ Disrespect Packet Today	2 Great Day ☆	3 ... Day ...
8 Great Day ☆	9 Great Day ☆	10 Rough Day ...	11 ... ☆
16 Great Day ☆	17 4th Small Attack E.R.	18 I Swearing packet	19
23	24	25	
29	30		

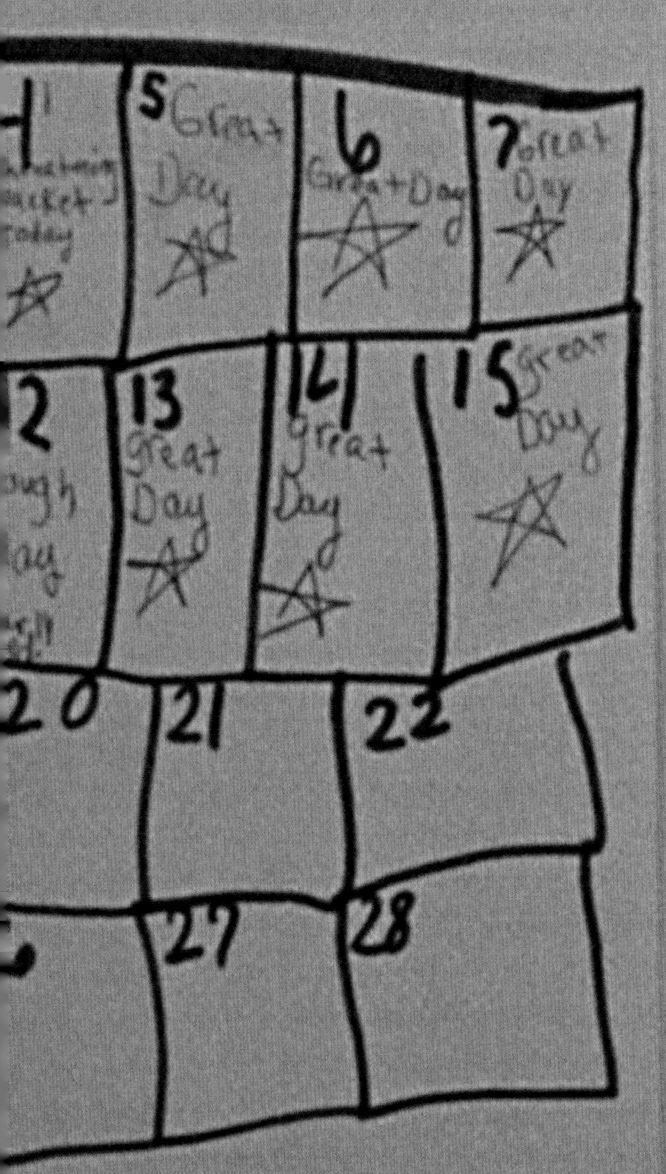

4
5 Great Day
6 Great Day
7 Great Day
12
13 Great Day
14 Great Day
15 Great Day
20
21
22
27
28

A.   Name - Barbara Goldin, born 5/21/46
        Age at Intake - (14)
        Age at Discharge - 14

        Placed at Bellefaire - 11/3/60
        Discharged - 1/16/61

        Family - Father - Herman Goldin, born 8/28/13
                 Mother - Lillian (Kantrovitz) Goldin, born 9/30/15.
        Address - 305 Belton Rd., Silver Springs, Md.
        Father's Occupation - Economist, Federal Communications Commission.

        Siblings - Stephen, born 8/28/48
                   Jonothan, born 2/18/51
                   Nancy, born 9/12/53

B.   Source of Referral - Jewish Social Service Agency, Washington,
                        D.C.. Referral for residential treatment
was made after a period of out-patient therapy. Barbara and her mother
had both been seen privately since 1/59.

C.   Reason for Referral - Barbara is described as having been a
                        "very quiet, submissive and compliant
child, affectionate, straight A student, and excellent pianist" until
the summer of 1958, about two years before referral. The onset of
acting out behavior occurred when she was age 12 and entering the
7th grade. She "suddenly" lost interest in studying and music and
became involved in severe behavior difficulties at home and in school -
open defiance, physical abuse of the mother, sexually provocative
behavior, and association with "undesireable" friends. She became
"loud and course" in speech, threatened to become a prostitute, and
lived only for Saturdays when she could "make out" with boys in the
movies. She and the mother engaged in constant physical and verbal
battles, with Barbara once throwing a knife at her mother.

The onset of difficulty is described as "sudden", but the history
reveals early facial tics, nervous mannerisms, headaches, sleeping
difficulties, fears of heights, bugs, and falling. There have also
been frequent accidents from age 3½, leg burns, falls from horses,
and at age 12, an unexplainable limp following the onset of the menses.

Both parents are highly intelligent but severely disturbed people who
come from emotionally and materially deprived backgrounds which they
seemed to strive to overcome through academic achievements. One of
the major difficulties was the destructive mother-daughter relationship
                                                    The mother sought to
succeed intellectually and socially thru Barbara and expected high
achievement from her,   The
mother saw B. as a "brilliant and artistic child" and felt that her
sudden change was "a tremendous waste of potential". The mother seemed
to identify B. with her own brother who became mentally disturbed, and

Mrs. Goldin frequently told B. that one of them would end up in a
mental institution. The mother also seemed to derive vicarious
satisfaction from B's acting out, referred to her as a whore, and
was unable to provide controls which Barbara desperately needed.

The father is a passive, remote man who was less directly involved
with B., but had outbursts of temper against her and wasalso unable
to control her. ██
██

At the time of referral, the home situation was one of chaos, with
B. holding the upper hand, and behaving in a manner contrary to the
conscious wishes of the family, but perhaps in accordance with the
████████ unconscious wishes. Tho B. was receiving treatment, there
was some question of how helpful this relationship was. She used
the therapist to help her fight her mother.

D.   The parents held custody of Barbara but custody was transferred to the Juvenile Court of Montgomery County prior to placement,
as a protection for the placement.

E.   On the day of placement, B. screamed and kicked and had to be
held to prevent her attack on her parents. She was immediately
hostile toward the Bellefaire staff and other children, insisted that
she would not remain here, used course language, and constantly
screamed and yelled. Underlying this acting out and air of defiant
bravado seemed to be a real panic and depression. When she was not
screaming, B. was pleasant, likable and appealing to both adults and
children.

Barbara was placed in the Bellefaire School. During her first week
here, she was seen for psychiatric evaluation, and on 11/30/60 began
weekly appointments with a caseworker. The parents were seen by the
referring agency, and there was some interference on the part of the
parents in that they wrote to Bellefaire, giving their ideas of B's
treatment, and <u>sent B. razor blades, medication, etc.</u> without con-
sulting Bellefaire.

F.   <u>Child's Use of Bellefaire</u> - Barbara's stay at Bellefaire was
                            brief. Her hostility toward the
placement continued unabated and her energy went into finding ways of
getting out of Bellefaire. She stated that she could not stand it
here and wanted to be sent to another institution. She regarded Blf.
as a mental institution and behaved as if she were in a mental institution, sometimes behaving in a way that made it necessary to put her
in a locked room. She was sexually provocative with the boys and con-
tinually attempted to promote struggles among staff members, as if she
were trying to recreate the destructive interaction she experienced at
home. She showed self-destructive tendencies in that she often cut
herself on the hands, face, and legs with a razor. <u>(Her mother sent her
a razor blade and followed them with a letter to the staff, wondering
if she should have sent it)</u>. Much of B's behavior was provocative
in attempting to involve other people in a struggle.

Barbara attended casework regularly, was not hostile to her caseworker, and seemed to have potential to relate well. One quality in this, as expected, was an attempt to set the caseworker up as an ally against the rest of the Bellefaire staff. However, she also seemed to show a real desire to be helped.

B. seemed to have an omnipotent feeling of being able to change her environment and her efforts were directed at getting out of Bellefaire. After one week here, she ran away, got as far as Pittsburgh, was returned to Bellefaire, but almost immediately attempted to run away again. She was then placed in Detention Home for a few days and returned to Blf. at her request. On 12/28/60, she again ran away after repeated threats to do this, went to a neighboring home, and asked to be returned to Blf.. Following her return, she refused to go to school, and her behavior necessitated putting her in a locked room in the infirmary during school hours. On the first day that this plan was terminated, B. made an attempt to attend school, did not feel able to remain there, returned to the cottage and setfire to her mattress and curtains, thus necessitating her return to the locked room, and the termination of her stay at Blf..

Our general impressions of B., in spite of her acting out behavior, were that she was <u>really a very frightened girl who attempted to handle her feelings through actions, who had an extremely destructive image of herself,</u> but underneath wanted controls and had potentialfor using treatment. No diagnosis was definitely determined, but the thinking was that this was a neurotic disturbance, rather than a delinquent character formation.

G.   <u>Reasons for Discharge</u> - Barbara was discharged following the fire setting because it was felt that Bellefaire could not continue with her in view of her resistance to being here and her need to behave uncontrollably in an attempt to get out of Blf..

She was discharged here to the court **and** referring agency for further planning. In view of our feeling that <u>she was a girl who had potential for using treatment constructively,</u> our recommendation was that she be placed in residential treatment in a very controlled setting, but with provision for treatment. One factor in her inability to use Blf. seemed related to unresolved problems in regard to the placement. Barbara had apparently been unclear as to the court commitment when she arrived here and obviously had not accepted the need to be placed so that there were difficulties in this respect from the very beginning.

Elizabeth Fleming
CASEWORKER

BF/mwc
3-10-61

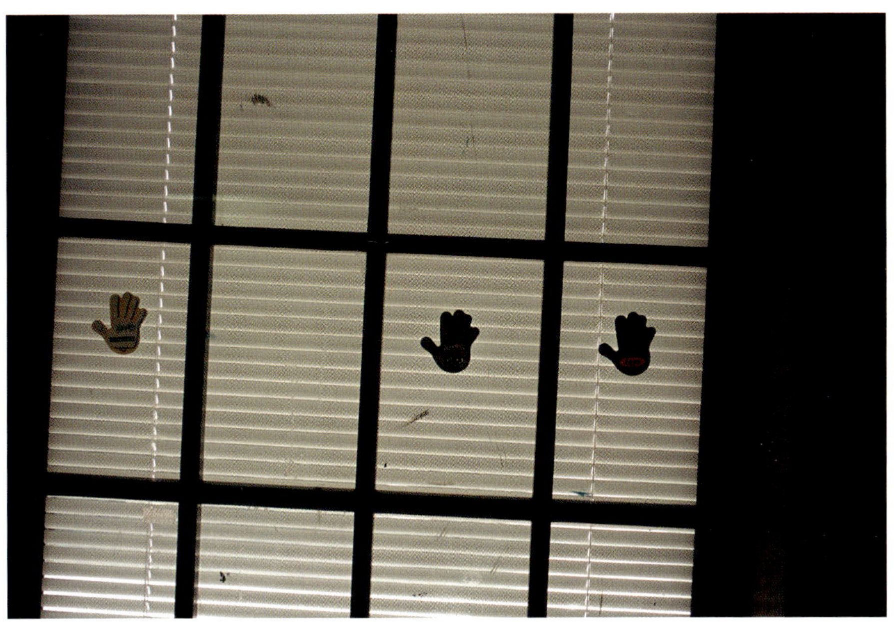

Bellefaire, Cleveland, Ohio, 2004

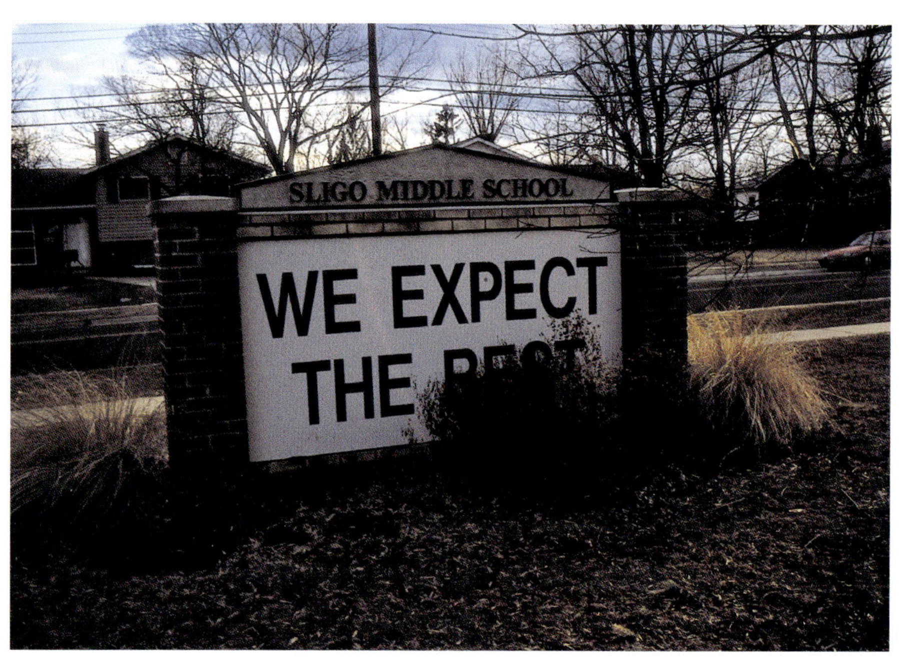

SLIGO SCHOOL, SILVER SPRING, MARYLAND, 2004

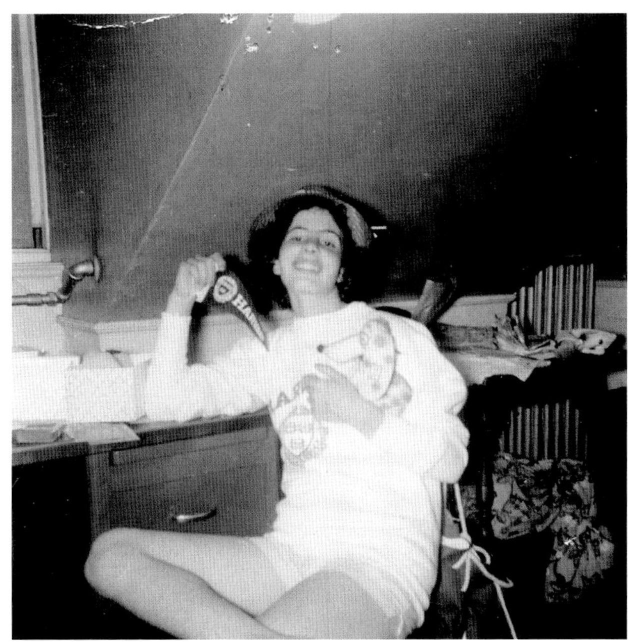

Barbara at home with Harvard banners, 1964

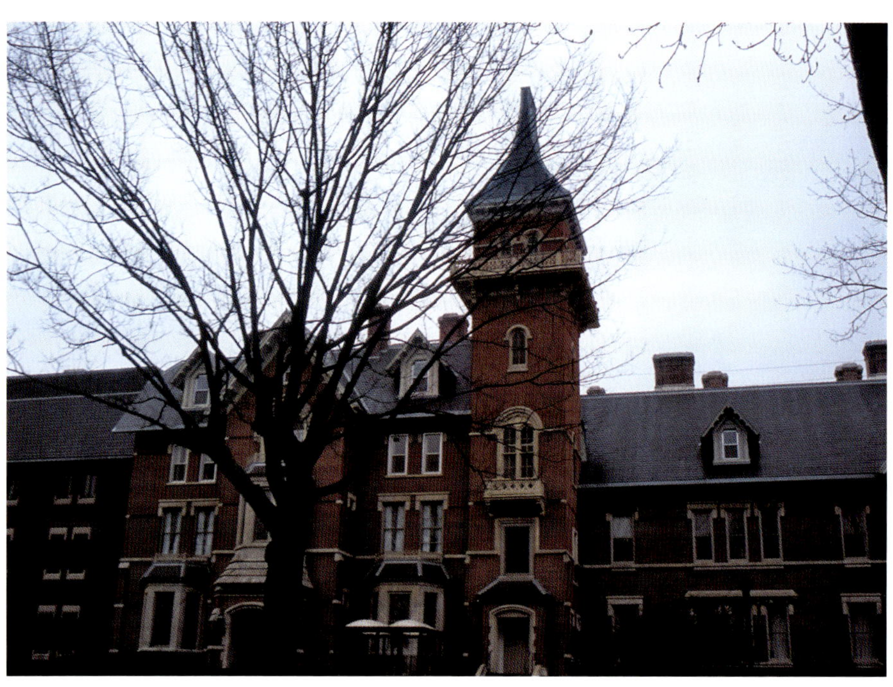

SHEPPARD PRATT HOSPITAL, BALTIMORE, MARYLAND, 2004

"She was put in the hospital because she had
a Negro boyfriend who was much older than her,
and her parents thought it inappropriate.
She met him at a professional wrestling match,
which she loved to go to. He was a boxer.
She referred to him as her tower of strength.
When the patient entered the hospital she
appeared to be quite confused about her sexual
identity. From what she has said, she seems to
be frightened about sexual activity, and describes
with horror the period during which she was
picking up boys. She also has some feelings about
becoming a queer, and described how she was
attracted to other girls.
She was rather awkward and ungainly.
She left her legs unshaven."

After different doctors' assessments of her,
they found that there was no diagnosis and
that her problem was adjustment to adolescence.
Nurse's notes: "Miss Goldin was returned
to the hall by means of a car when she
attempted to escape from the Ford building.
She stated at that time, 'I'm going home, but I don't
have a home. I don't have anything or anybody'.
The mother would like us to simply tell
the patient that she is not well enough to be
outside of the hospital. When actually there is
much evidence to suggest that it's not Ms Goldin
who should be in the hospital, it's Mrs Goldin."

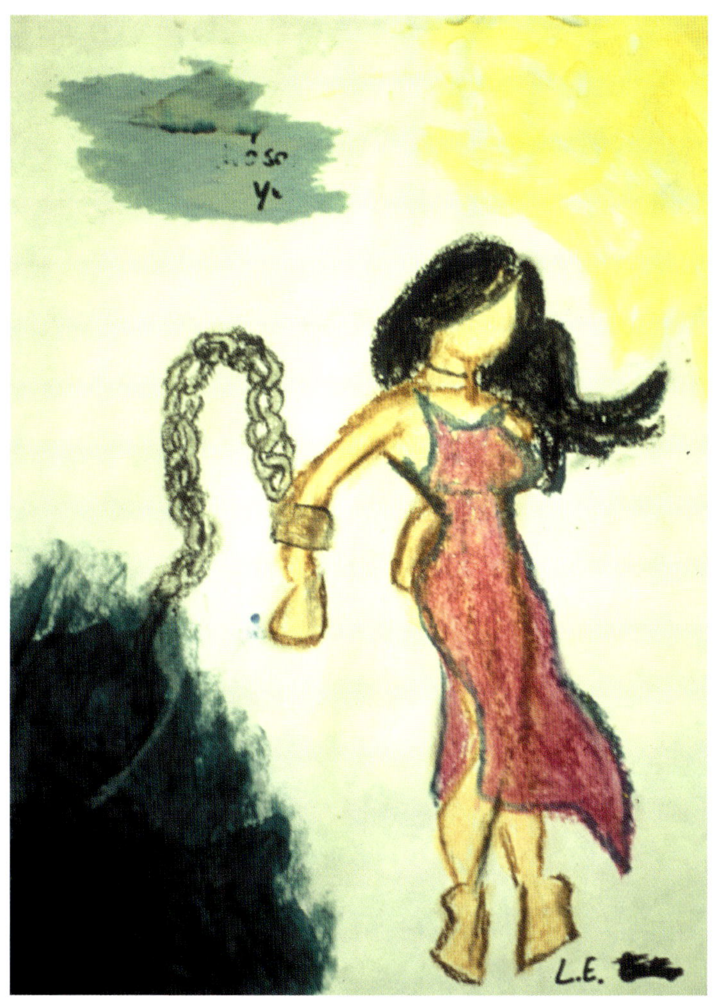

Sheppard Pratt Hospital, Baltimore, Maryland, 2004

Next page: Empty bed in locked ward
Sheppard Pratt Hospital, Baltimore, Maryland, 2004

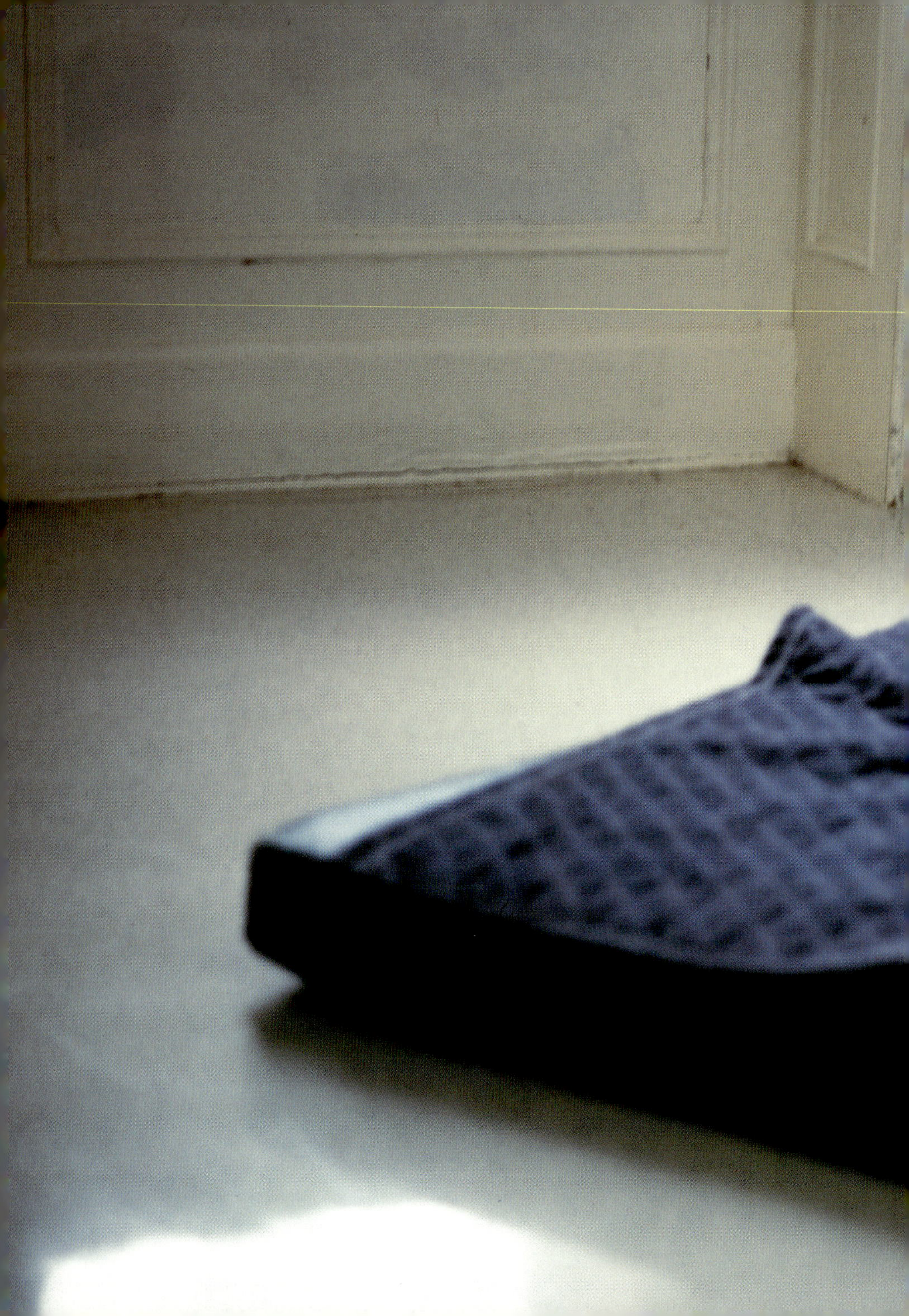

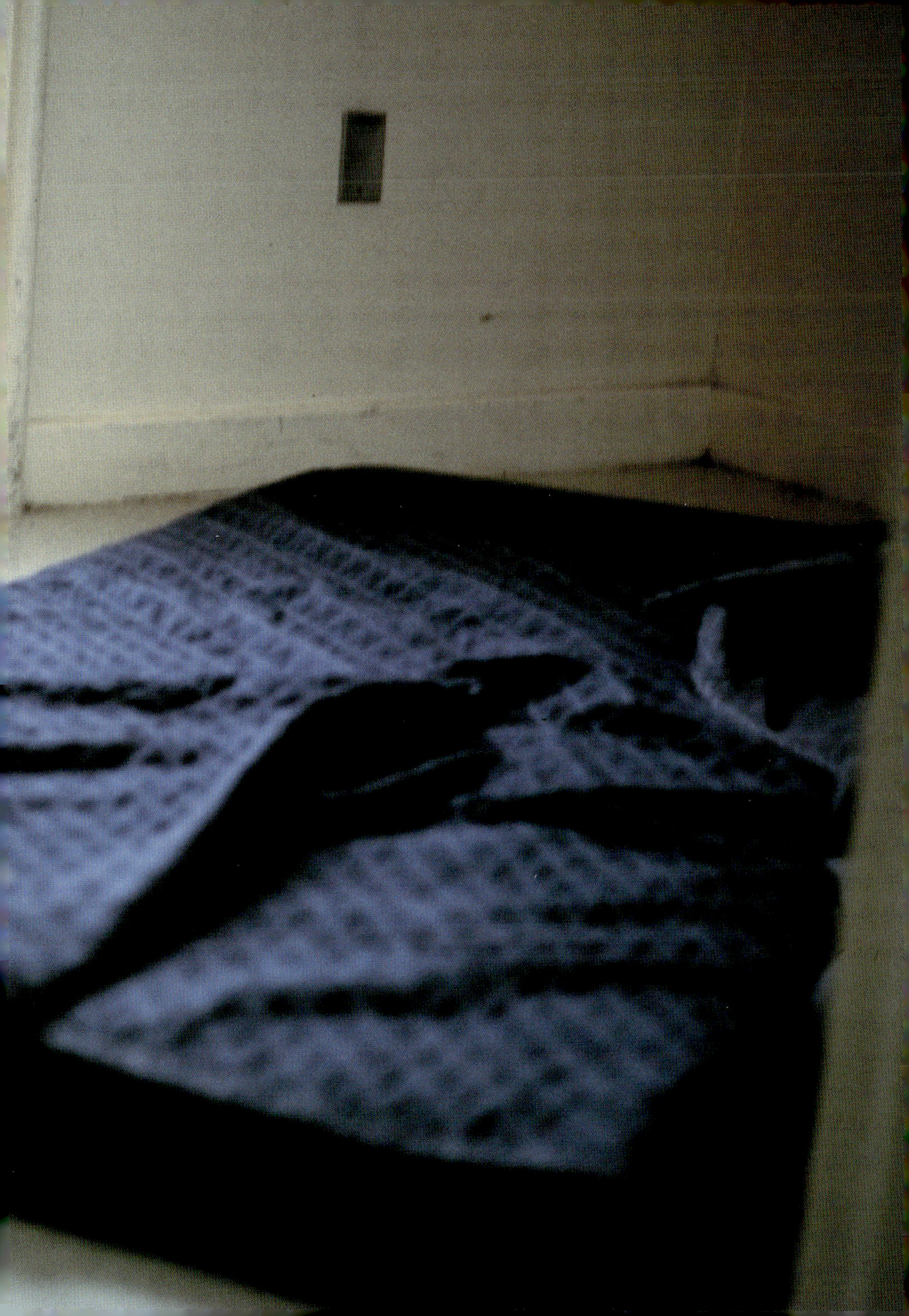

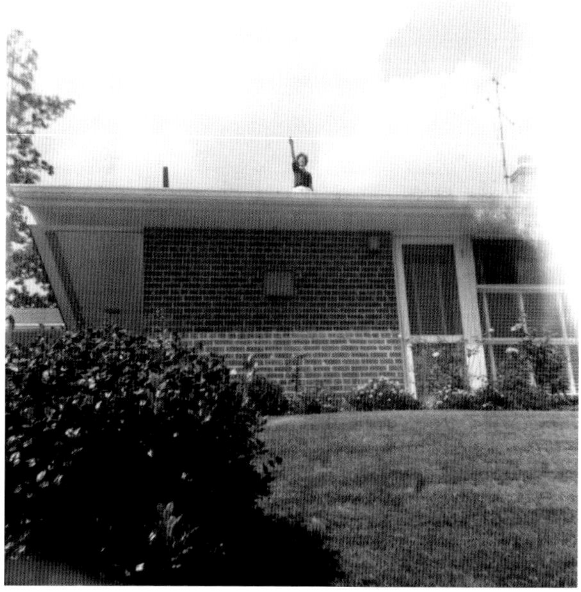

BARBARA ON TOP OF THE ROOF, SILVER SPRING, MARYLAND, 1962

Course in Hospital – From February 18, 1962 to April 17, 1962):
As the patient's story began to develop, she saw her difficulties as centering around
an intolerable situation at home. Her fury seemed to be mainly directed at the
mother and yet expression of this was something she fought to avoid. She spoke
of her parents as being wonderful and yet at other times, she came close to cursing
them. She is, however, quite dependent on them. During the visits with the parents,
she has often become irate at them and on two occasions has slapped both the mother
and the father. Occasionally, she will state that she feels other patients on the
floor are after her and then will say that this is "crazy". She talks frequently of
having a nervous breakdown but so far has been able to remain on the admission hall.
At one time, she had general permission but this was cancelled after she reportedly
stated that she was going to escape.

The patient seems to have a great deal of warmth and ability to
relate in a meaningful way to other patients and the staff. She saw the writer as
being helpful but at the same time, said it would take years to work out her
problems and she did not want to talk about them anyway since if she did, she might
become "worse". She was told on the 16th of April that she would be transferred to
another doctor. She became quite tearful and began to suck her thumb and was unable
to speak. The outlook at the time of this note is one of hopeless anguish and yet
occasionally, she will describe happy experiences.

The patient was transferred on the 17th of April to Dr. Ciboles

E. Vidaud.

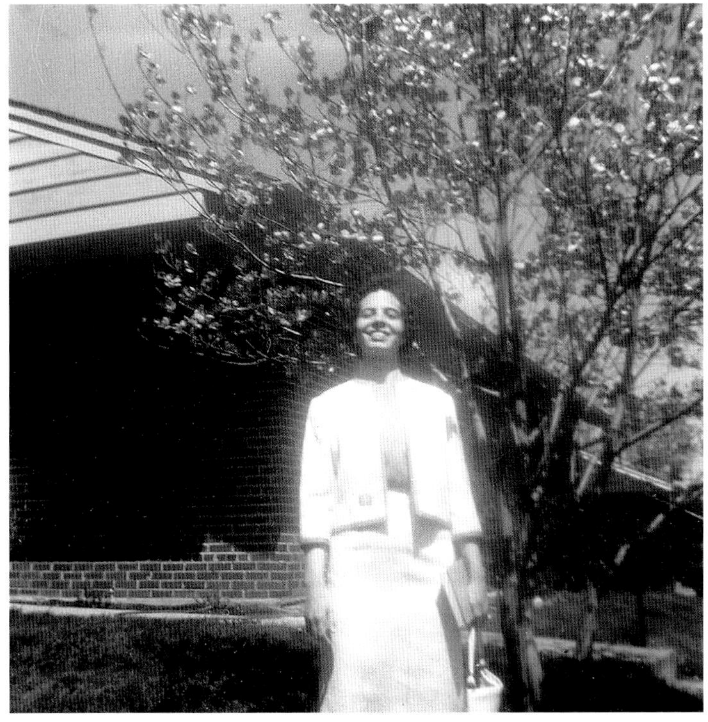

Barbara in front of the family house, April 1963

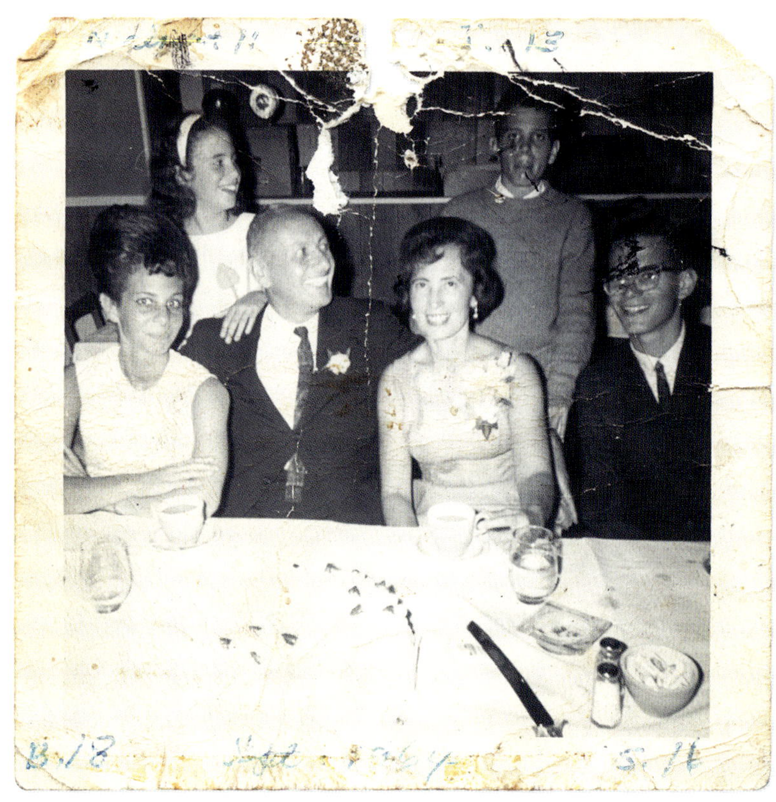

Family dinner, 1965

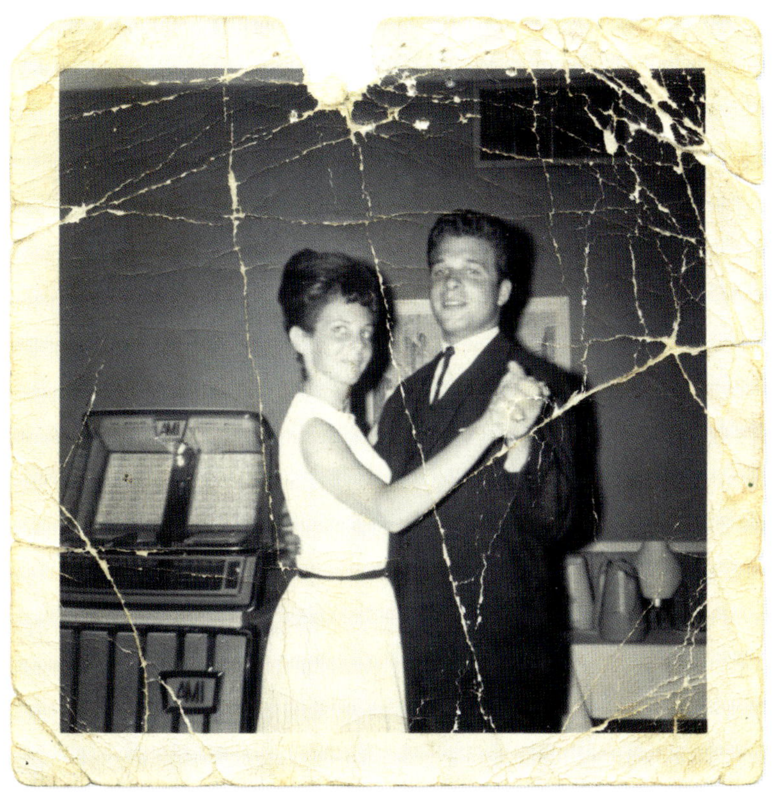

Barbara dancing with Victor, 1965

From the National Institute
of Mental Health in Washington:
"The patient presented a moderately attractive,
extremely tense young female, who spoke
in a somewhat affected, high-pitched tone
of voice, with occasional stammering.
There were a few scratches on the left wrist,
which were self-inflicted. After awhile she
began going on pass to arrange for tutoring
and also to look for employment."

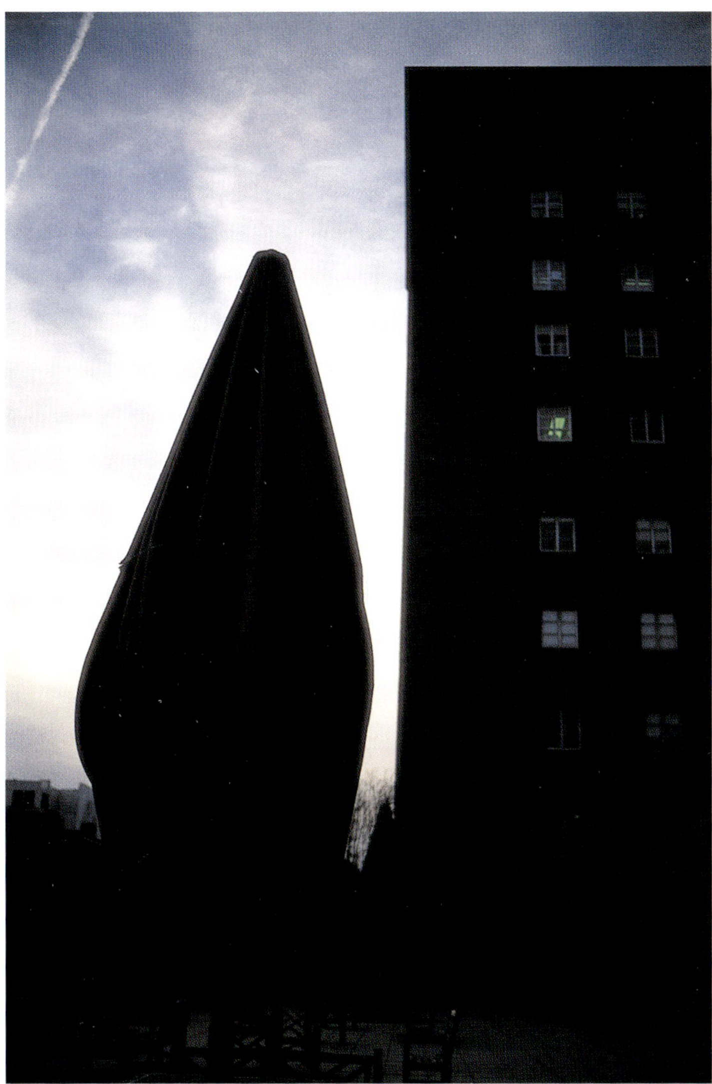

N.I.M.H., Washington, D.C., 2004

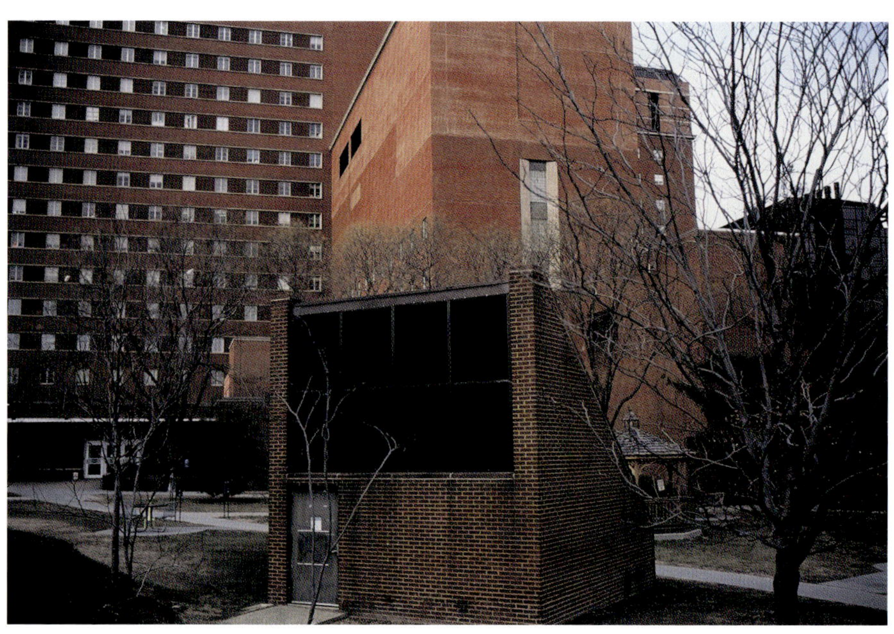

N.I.M.H., Washington, D.C., 2004

"On one occasion she was late from pass, and after returning said she wanted to leave against medical advice. She claimed that she wanted to be sent to a state hospital and be locked up. She changed her mind and decided to stay in treatment. On one occasion, she unprovokedly assaulted her mother, eventuating in a minor fracture in one of her mother's fingers. She claimed that she did in fact want to try to achieve something in her life, and felt that perhaps she could learn to get along with her parents."

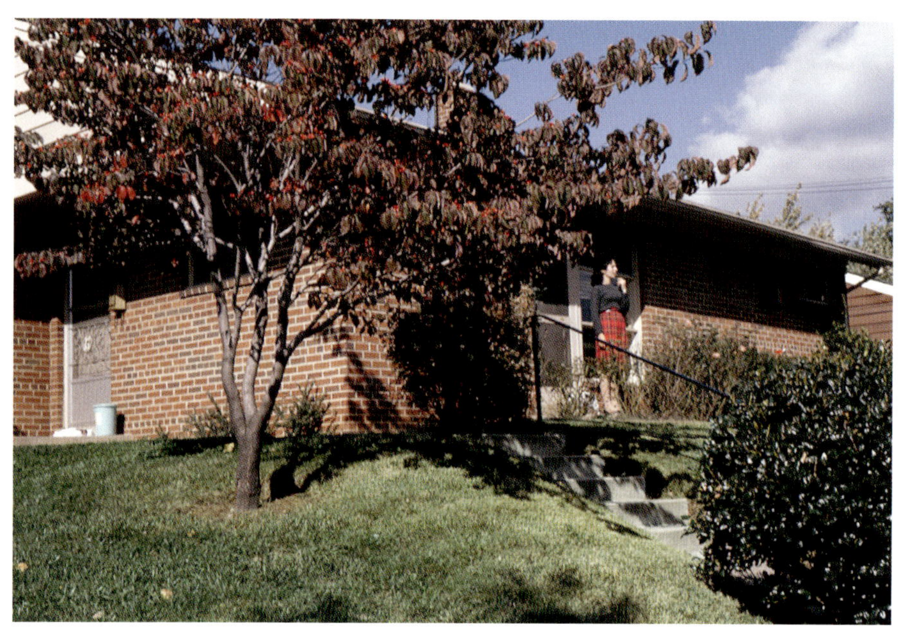

Barbara in front of the family house, Silver Spring, Maryland, 1964

On April 12, 1965, she was given
a pass in the morning to look for
employment in the community, and possibly
to stop at home to pick up some clothes.

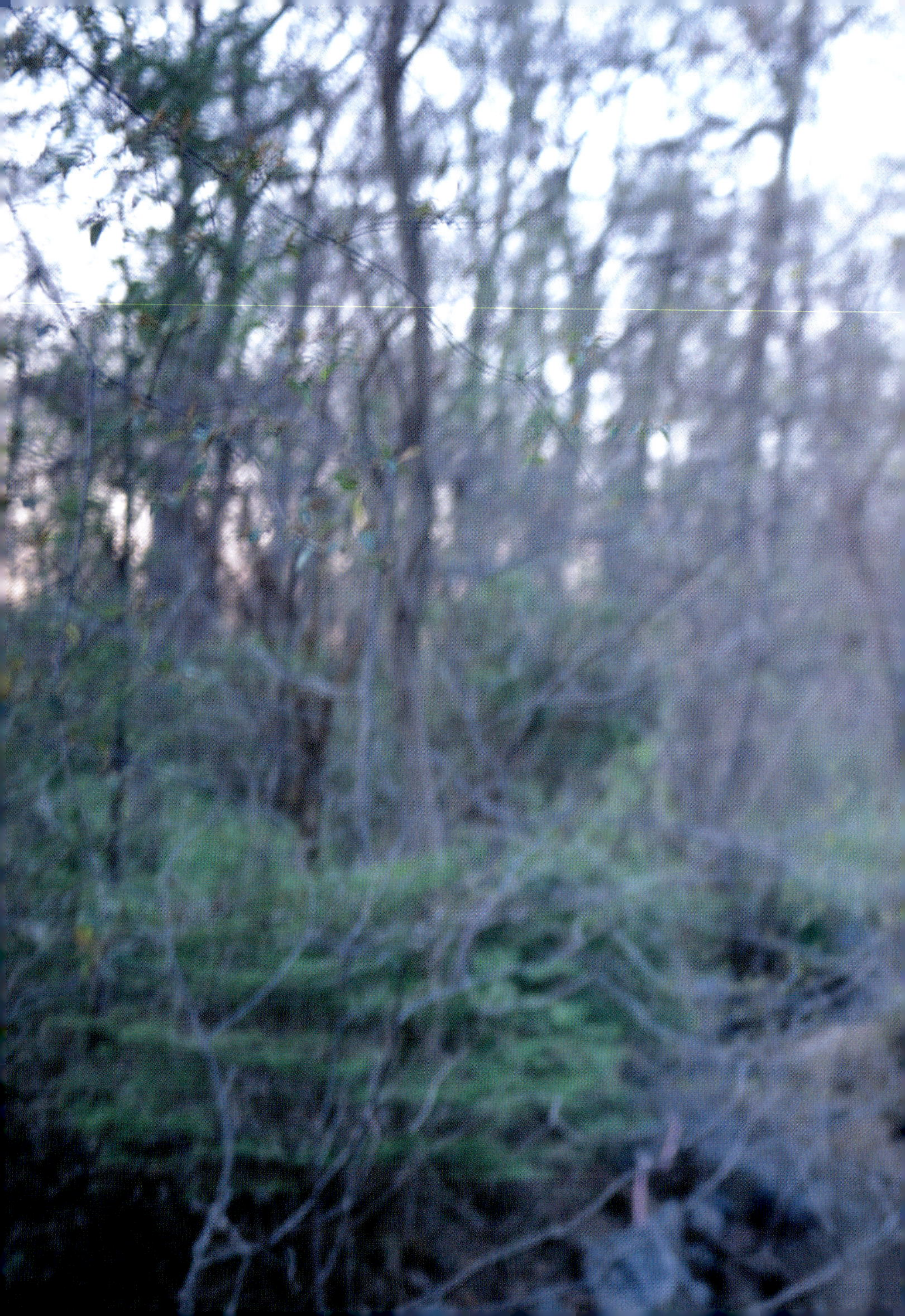

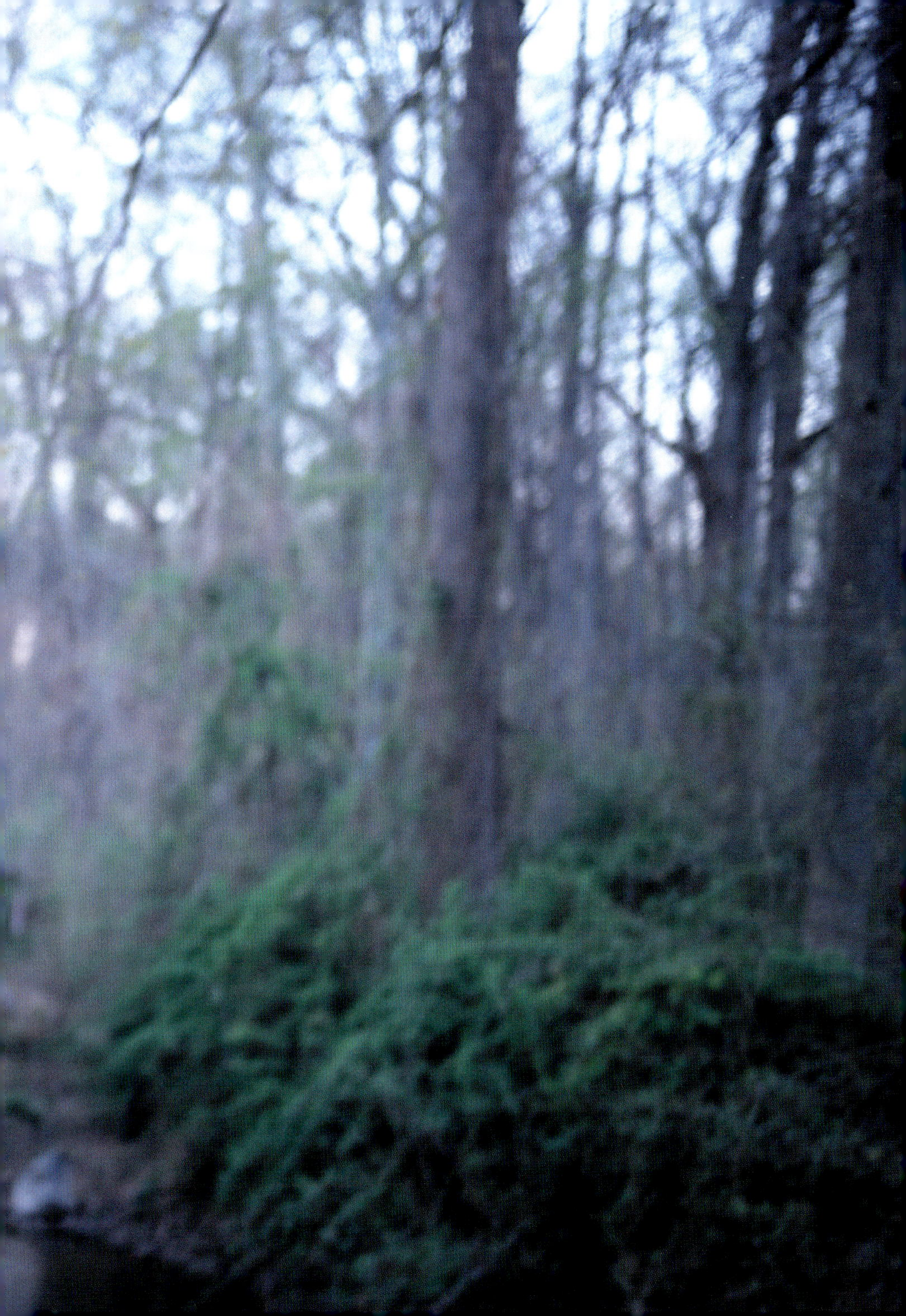

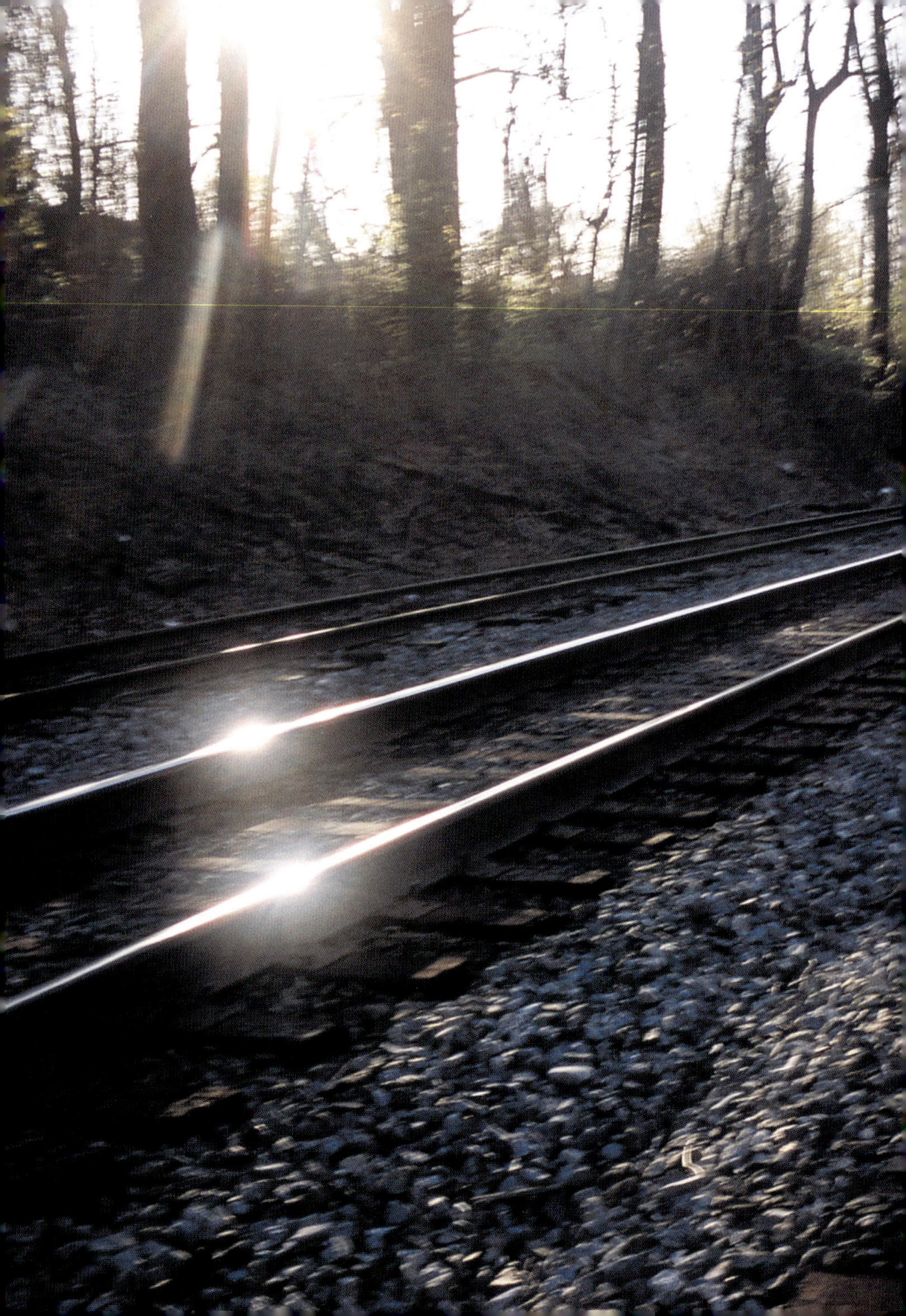

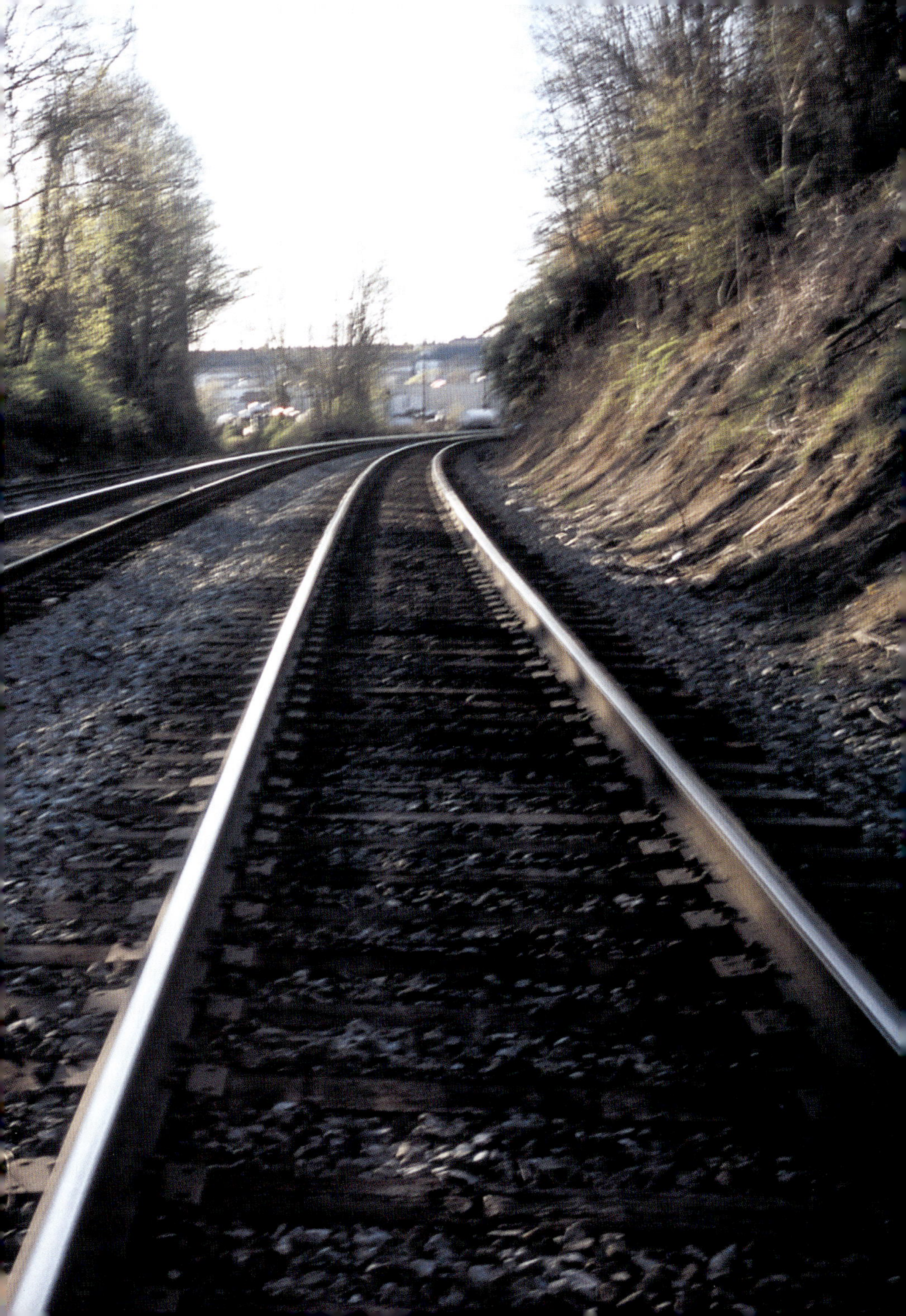

"Persons in the area told police they had seen
Miss Goldin a short time before, when she
asked when the next train was due to pass.
Shortly before 5:30 pm, persons said Miss Goldin
put her pocketbook on the ground next to the
tracks, then laid down across the tracks as
the 'Capitol Limited' approached. The train's
engineers told police they saw her and nailed
the brakes, but were unable to stop the train.
Police said the train ran over the girl and
dragged her body about 300 feet. Pathological
examiners ruled her death as a suicide.
Other significant conditions contributing
to death: severe mental depression."

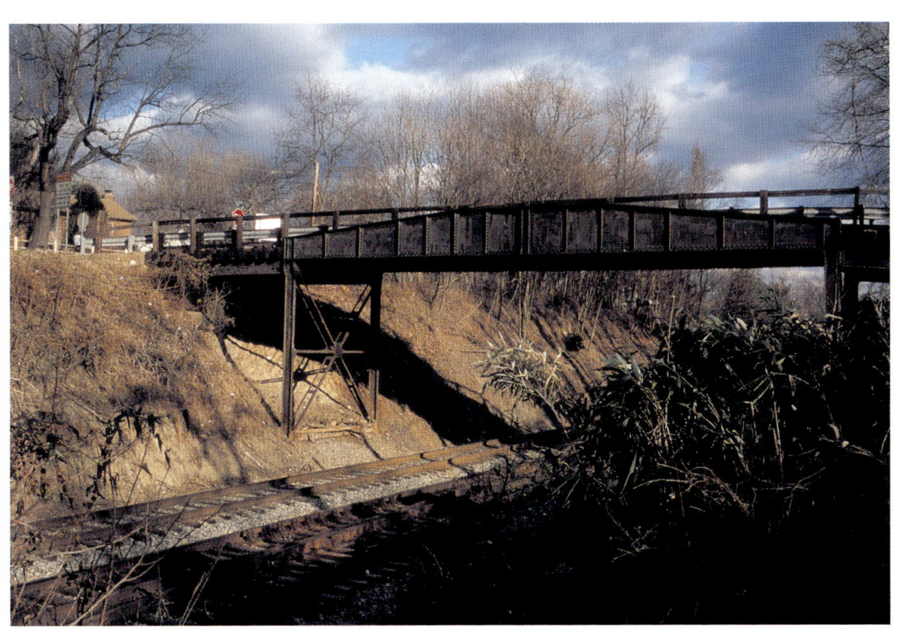

Bridge over train tracks, near Grace Church Road Overpass, Montgomery County, 2004

Girl Ends Life Under Train on B&O Tracks

Barbara Goldin, 18, of 305 Belton rd., Silver Spring, was killed yesterday afternoon when she was struck by the B&O's Capital Limited passenger train near the Grace Church Road overpass, according to Montgomery County police. She was the daughter of Mr. and Mrs. Hyman Goldin.

County police said the engineer and fireman reported they saw the girl step onto the tracks at about 5:40 p.m. and lie down in the path of the Washington to Chicago train. The engineer tried unsuccessfully to stop, police said, though the train was moving at a reduced speed.

Dr. Beldon Reap, County Medical Examiner, ruled the death a suicide. Police said no note was found.

Following the Capital Limited was a special Shenandoah Downs train, which was carrying 200 racing fans to Charles Town, W.Va. Delayed in Silver Spring, the train was 30 minutes late, causing the passengers to miss the daily double.

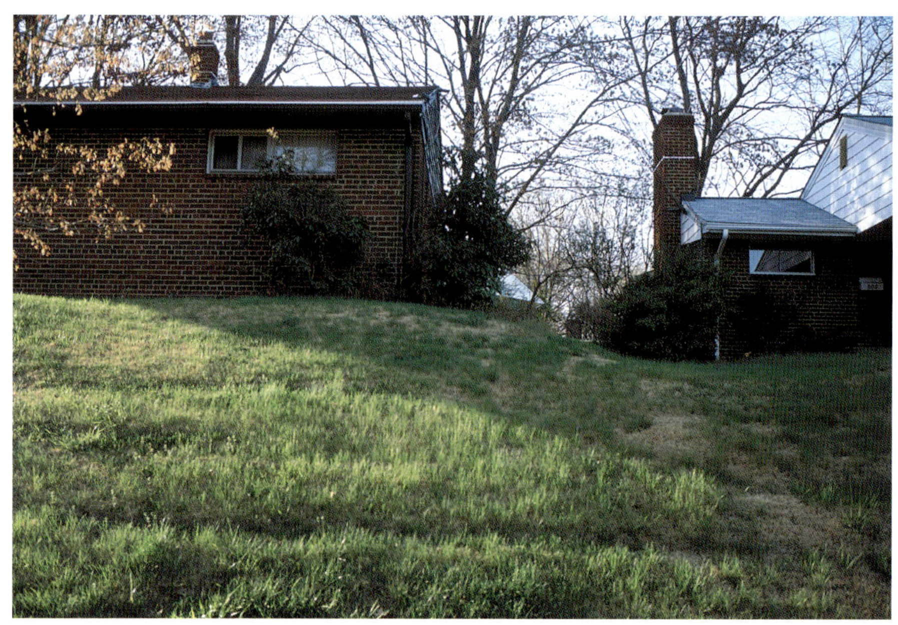

Family house, 305 Belton Rd, Silver Spring, Maryland

I heard my father screaming on the lawn.

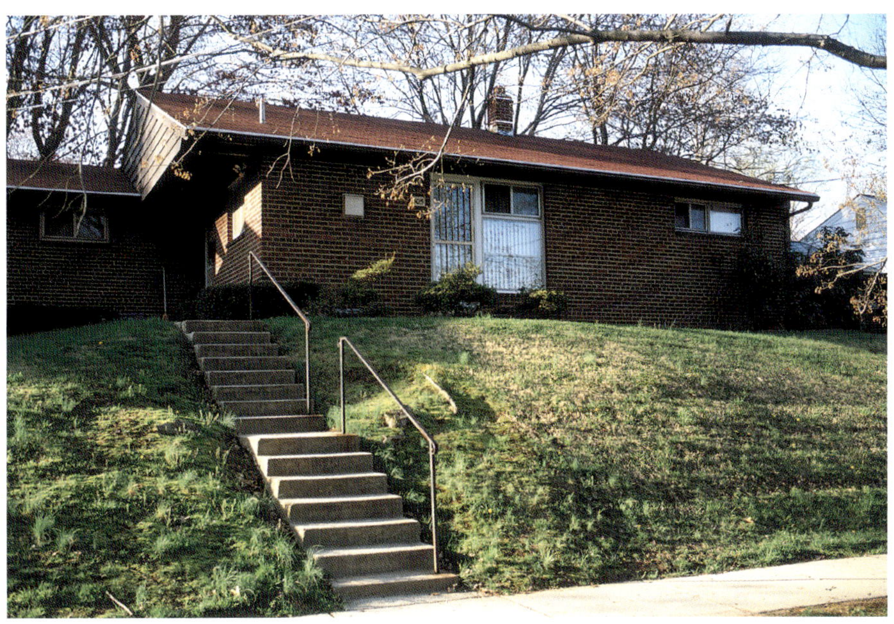

Family house, 305 Belton Rd, Silver Spring, Maryland

I heard my mother say to the policemen:
"Tell the children it was an accident."

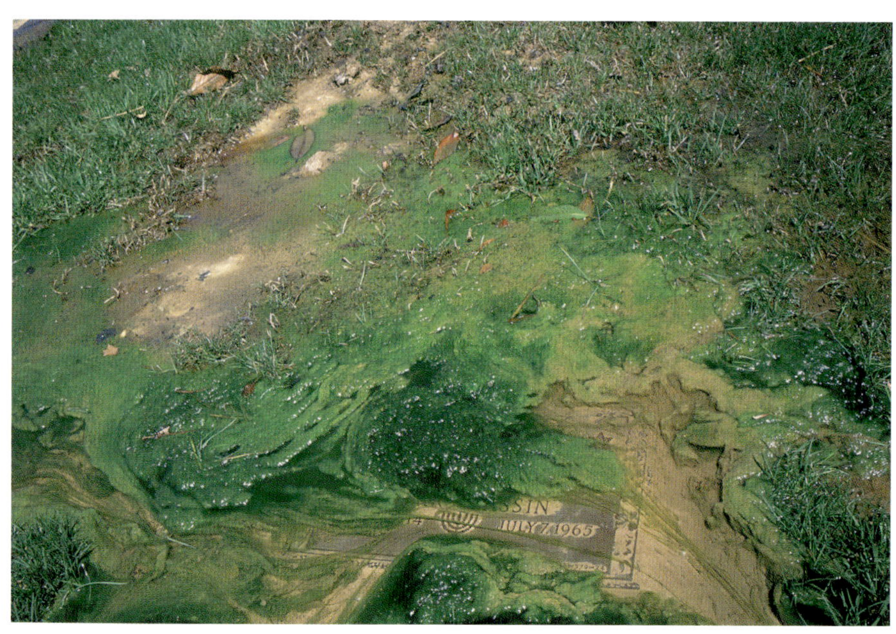

Graveyard flooded, King David Cemetery, 2004

FOUND IN HER PURSE. IT'S FROM JOSEPH CONRAD.

*Droll thing life is, that mysterious
arrangement of merciless logic for futile purpose.
The most you can hope for is some knowledge
of yourself that comes too late – a crop
of inextinguishable regrets.*

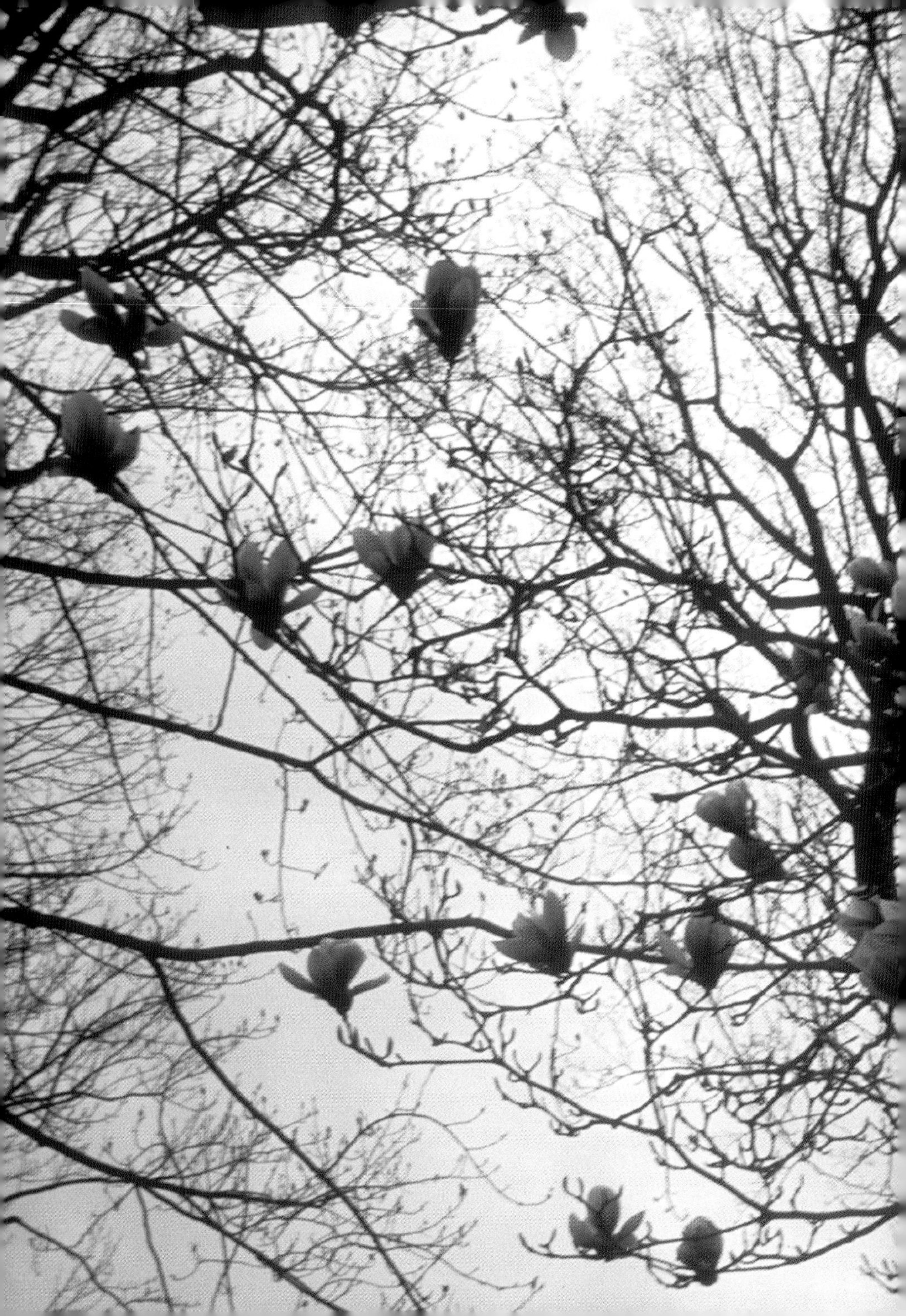

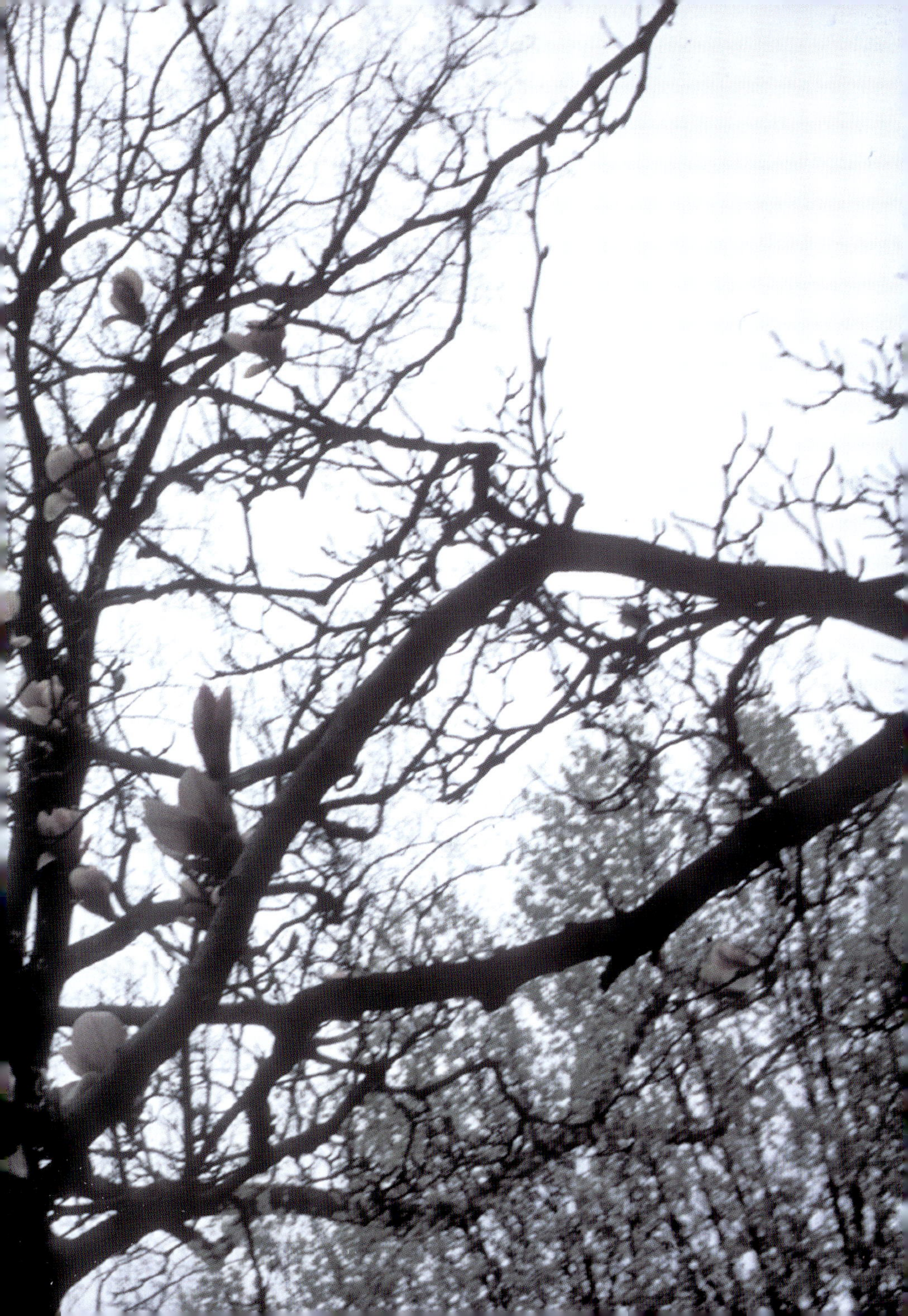

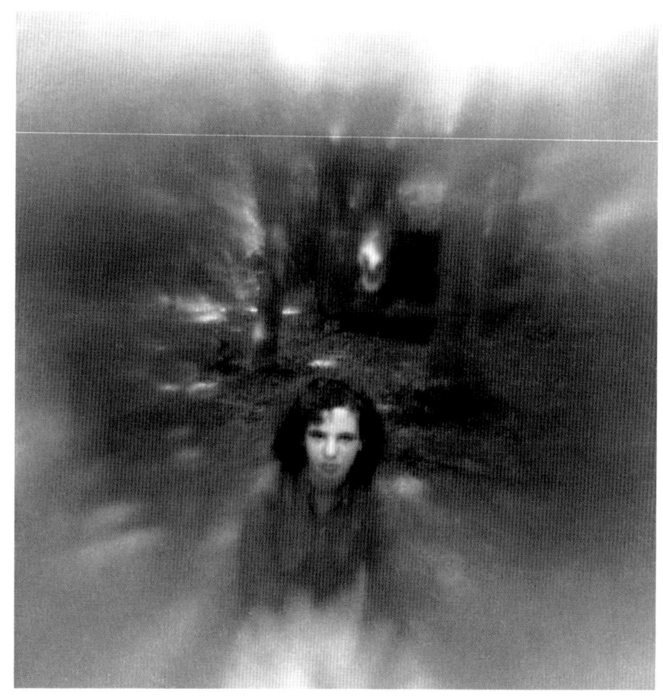

Nan, 1969

My sister told me her psychiatrist said
I would end up like her.
I thought I had to kill myself at 18.

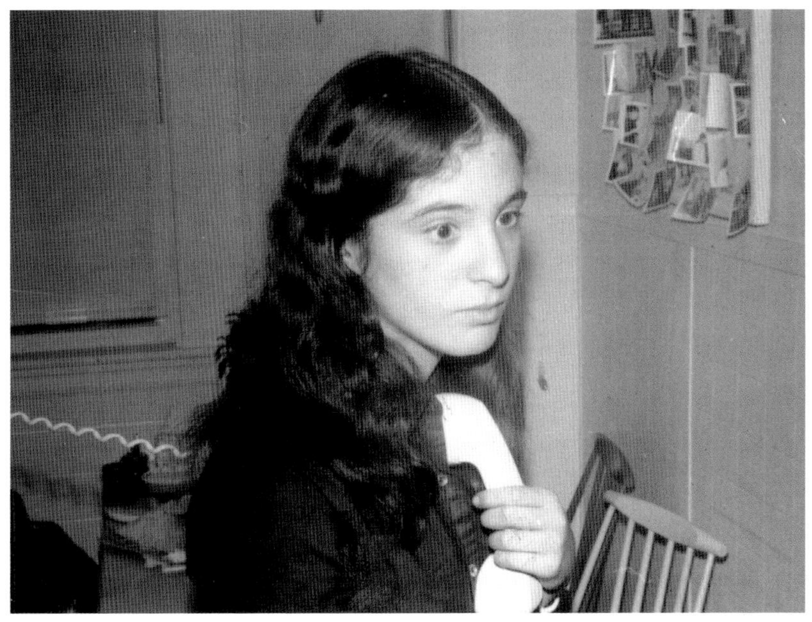

MY PARENTS STARTED TO TREAT ME LIKE BARBARA.

AT 13 I WANTED TO GROW UP TO BE A JUNKIE.

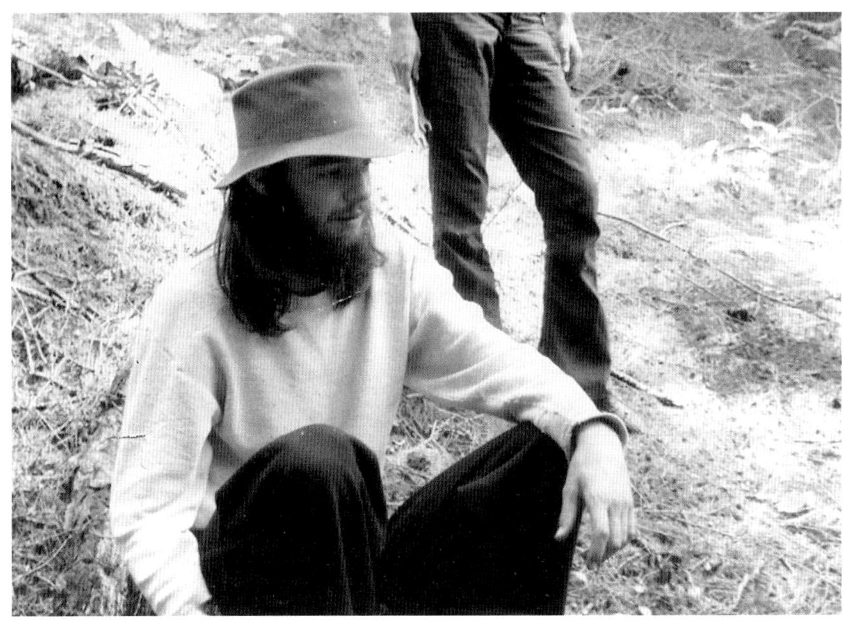

WOLFER, SATYA COMMUNITY SCHOOL, LINCOLN, MARYLAND, JULY 1969

AT 14, I LEFT HOME.

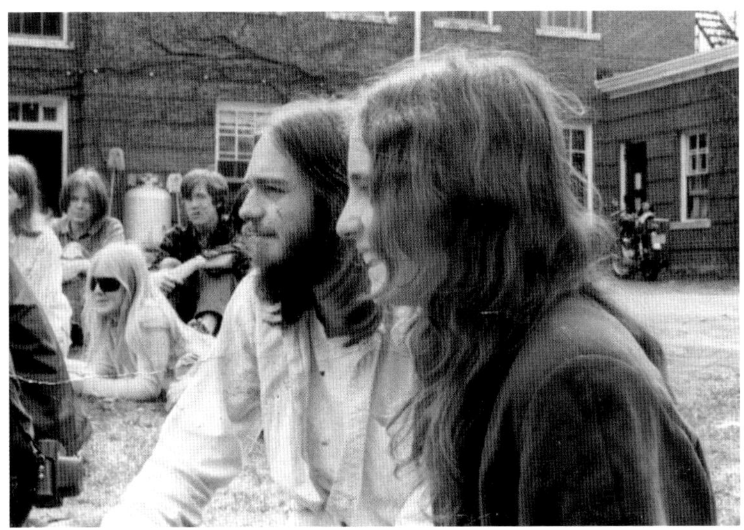

Nan and Wolfer, Satya Community School, Lincoln, Maryland, July 1969

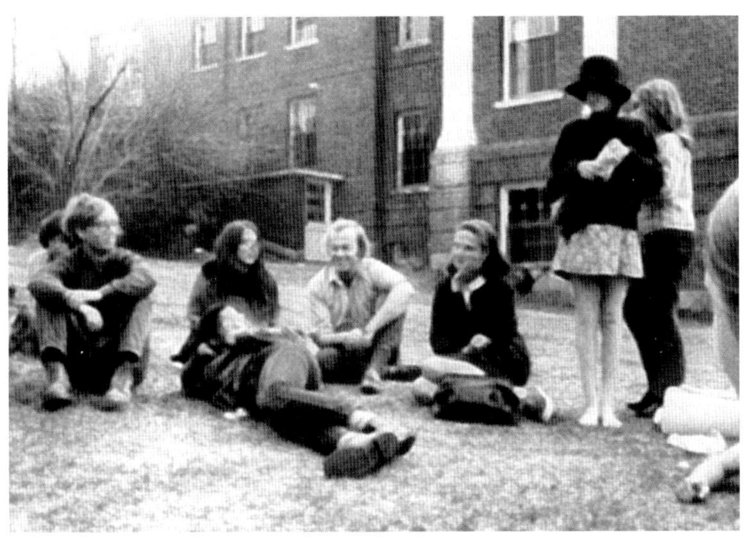

Satya Community School, Lincoln, Maryland, July 1969

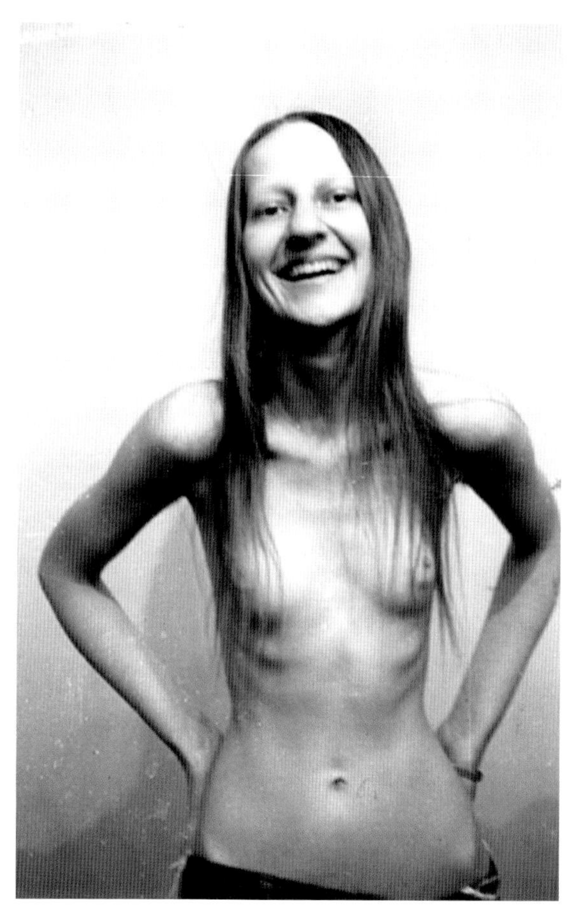

Suzanne nude, Fayette St, Boston, 1971

AND THEN I FOUND MY OWN FAMILY.

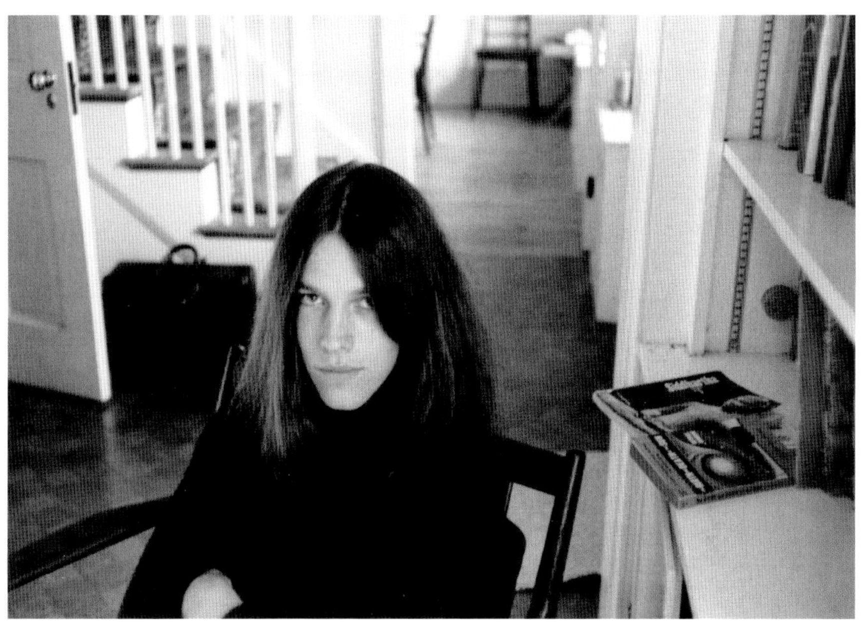

THESE WERE THE FIRST TWO FRIENDS I PHOTOGRAPHED.

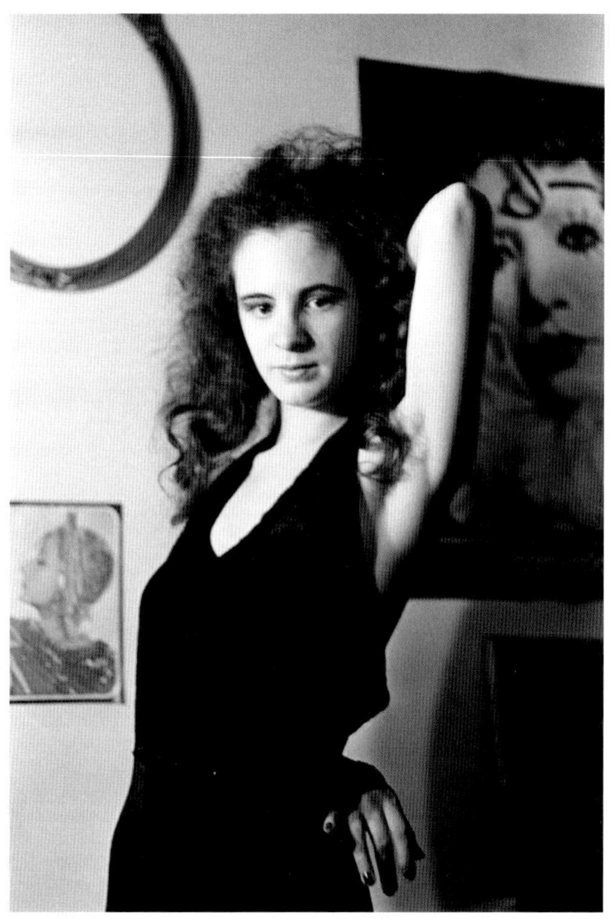

Nan in a velvet gown, Fayette St, Boston, 1971

At 18 I started to shoot dope, and shoot
pictures. That saved my life.

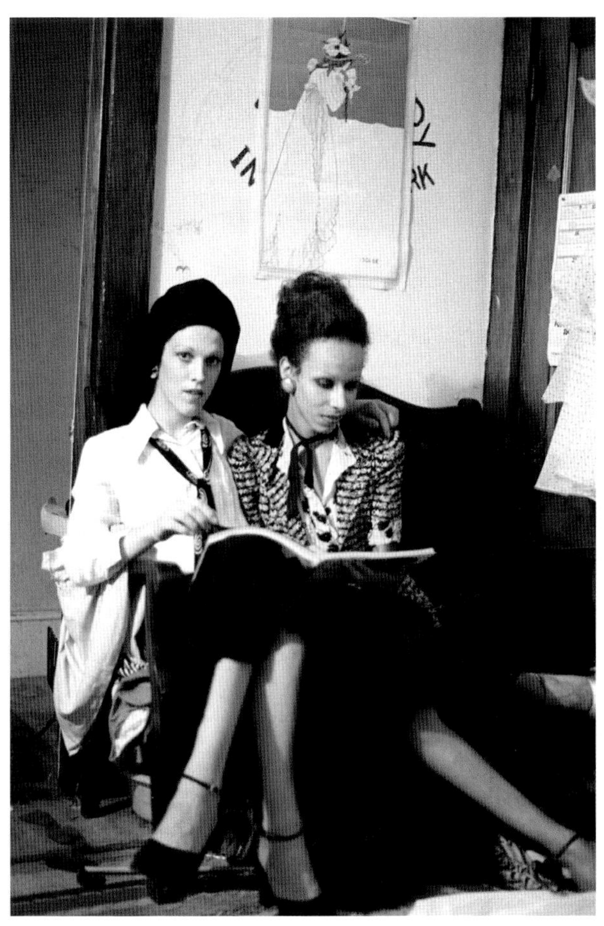

DAVID AND BEA AT HOME IN PARISIAN DRAG, MASSACHUSETTS, 1971

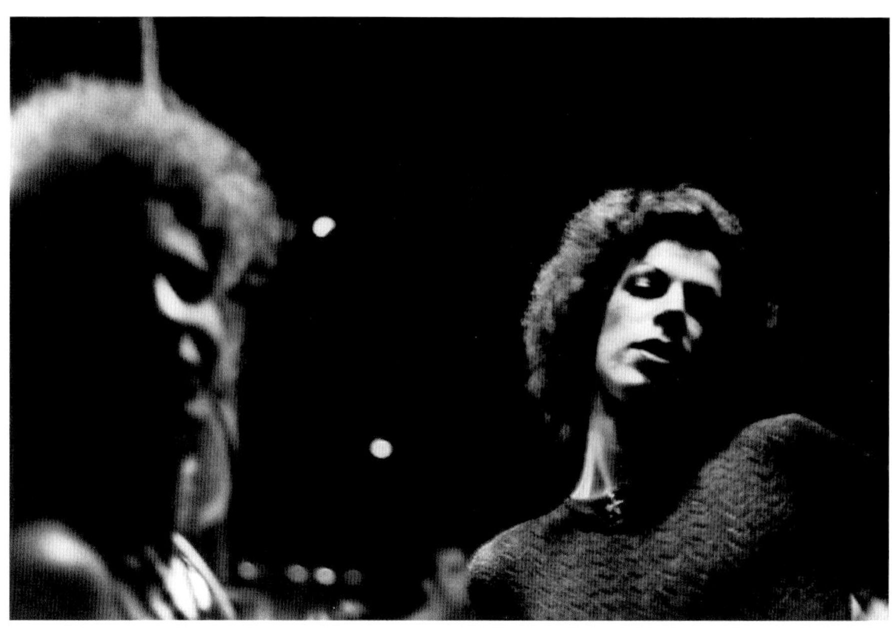

Nan and Ivy at a party, Beacon Hill, Boston, 1972

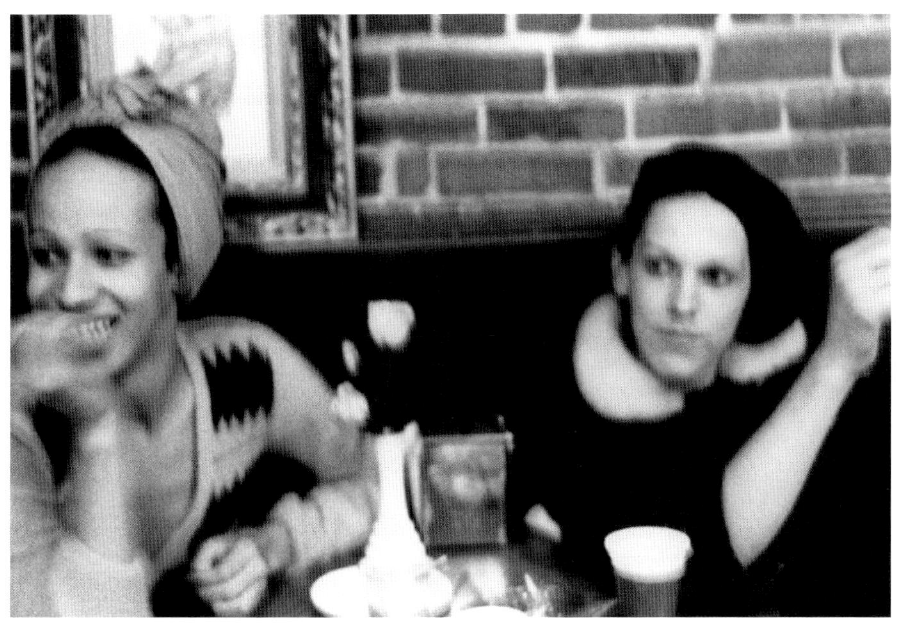

BEA AND DAVID AT A CAFÉ, CHARLES ST, BOSTON, 1972

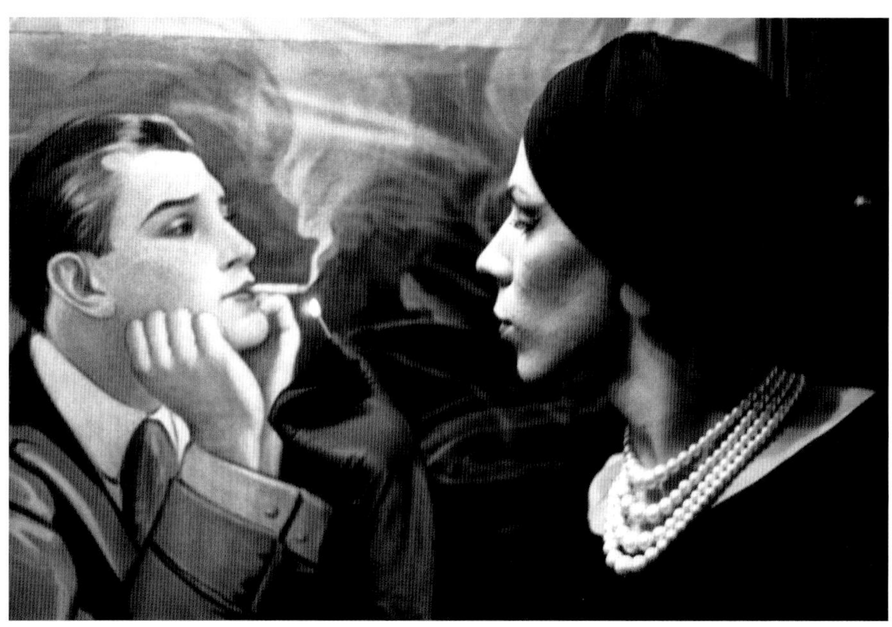

CHRISTMAS AT THE OTHER SIDE, BOSTON, 1972

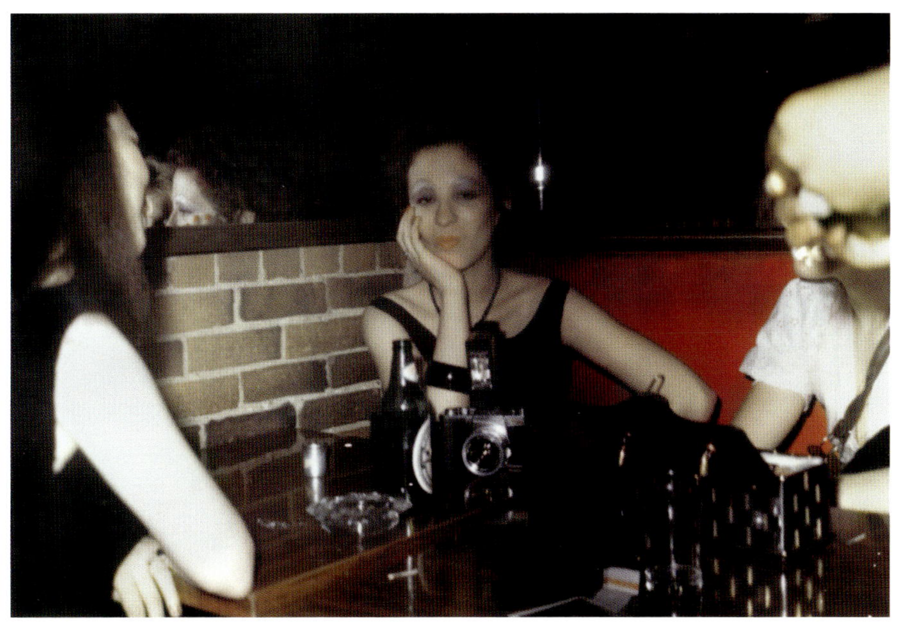

NAN WITH SUSAN AND LOLA, THE OTHER SIDE, BOSTON, 1973

DRUGS GAVE ME MY SOCIAL PERSONALITY.

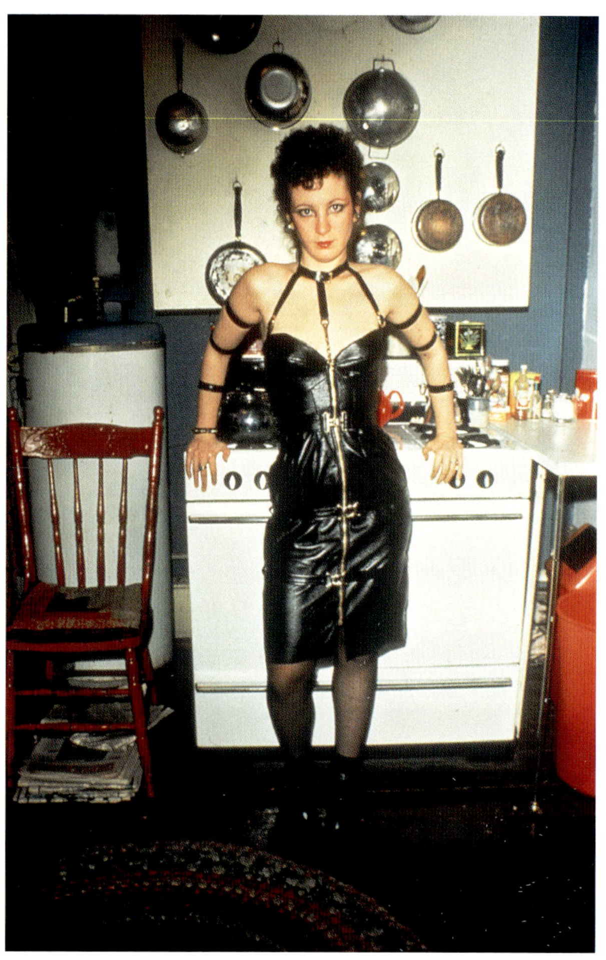

NAN AS A DOMINATRIX, BOSTON, 1978

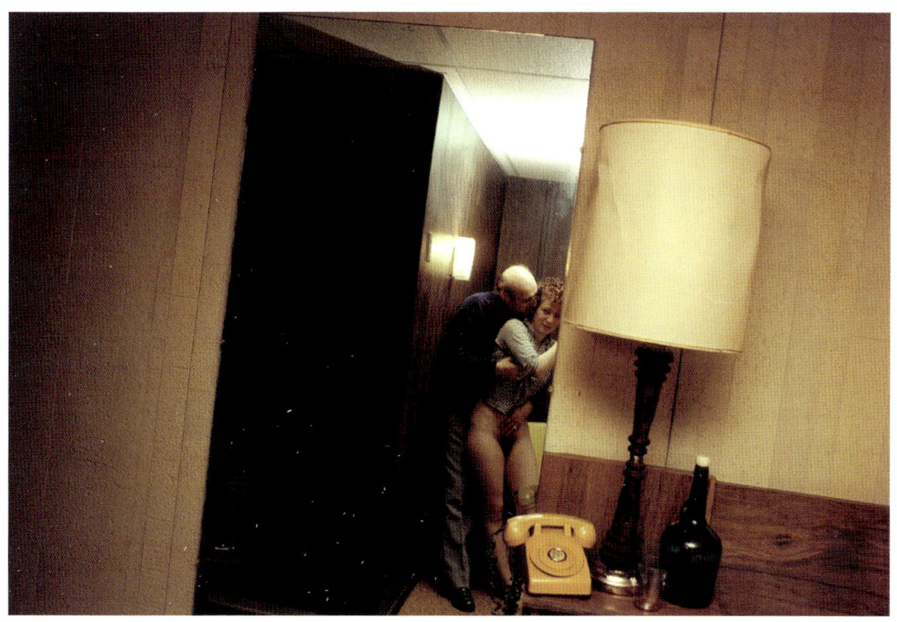

Nan and Dickie in the York Motel, New Jersey, 1980

Next pages: Nan and Brian in bed, NYC, 1983

Nan at the hospital, Berlin, 1984

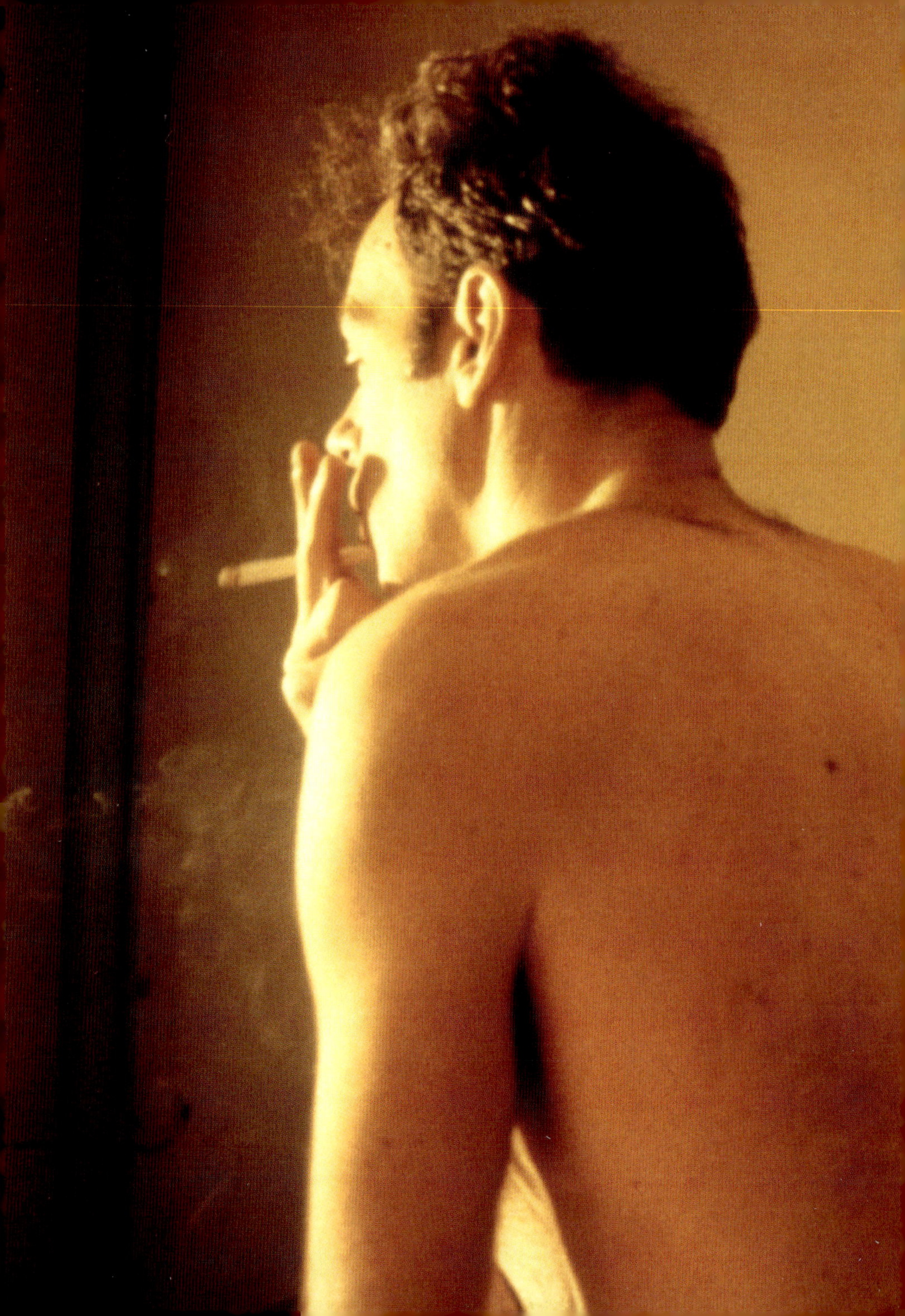

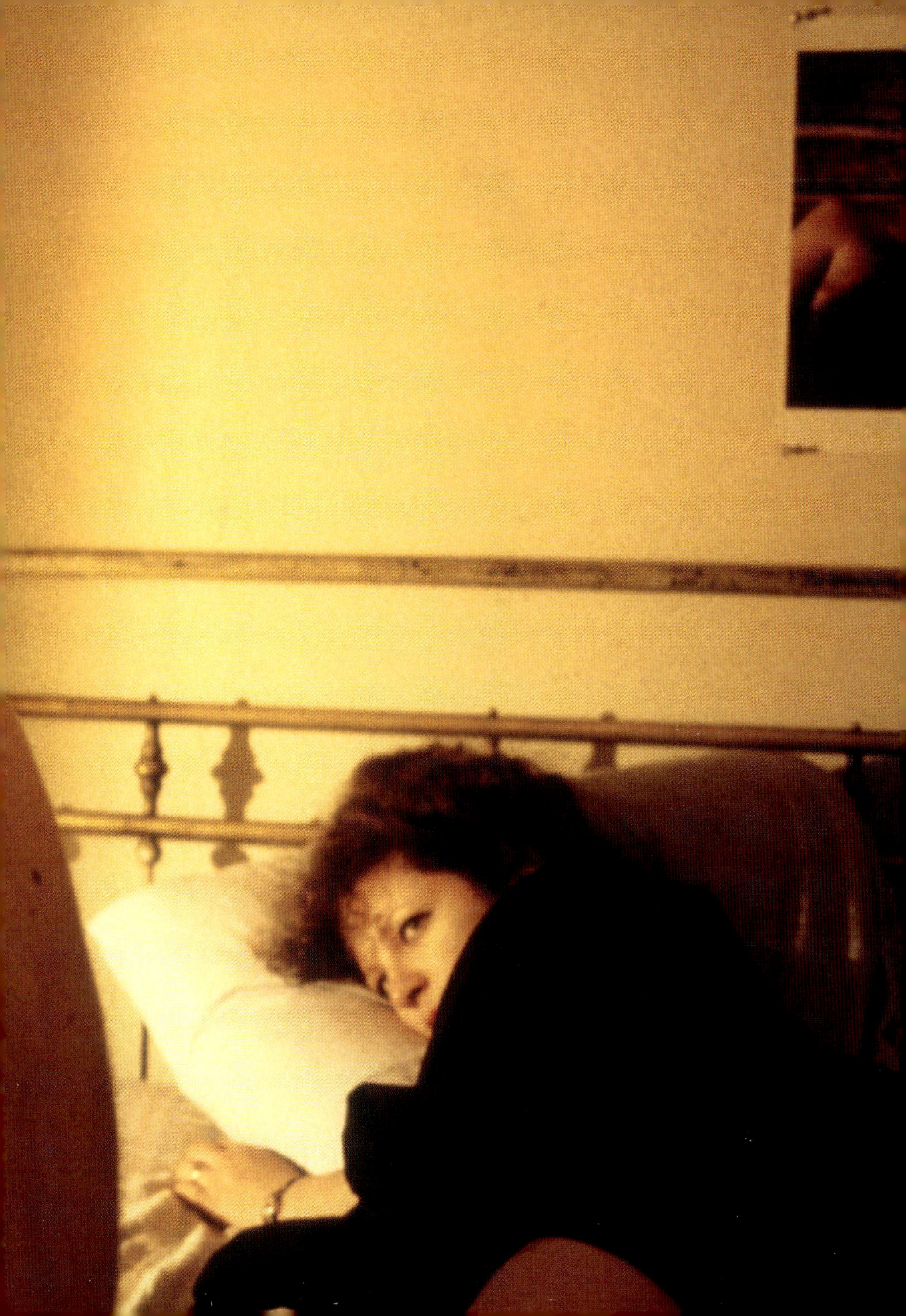

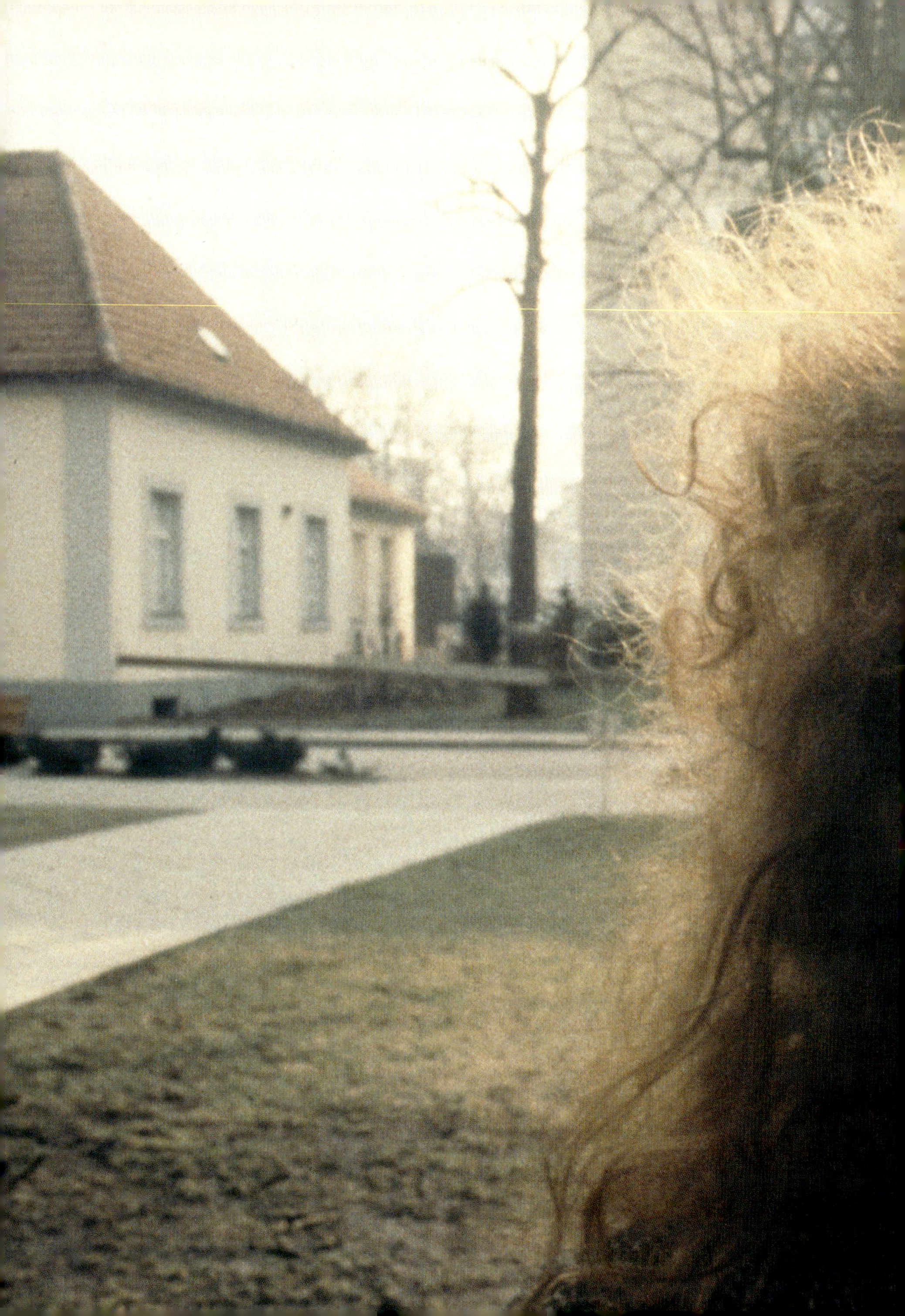

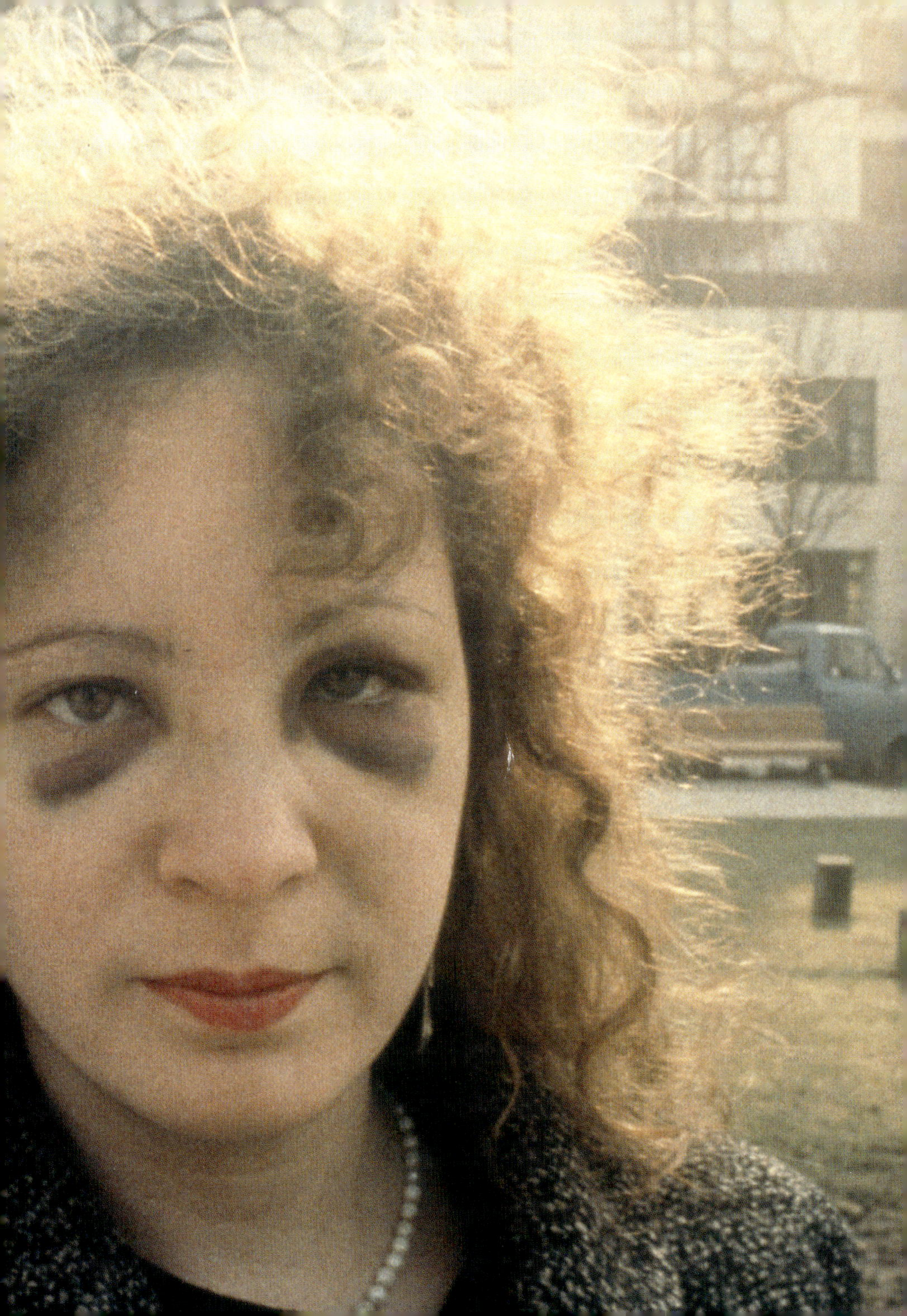

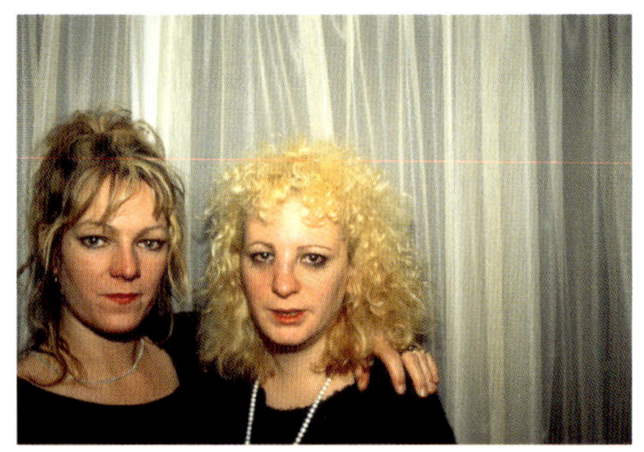

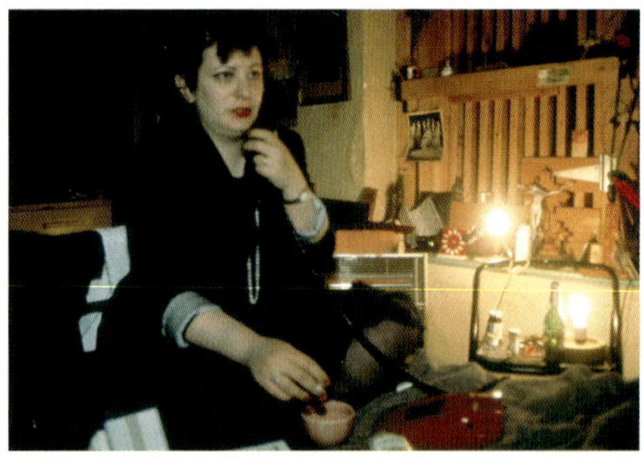

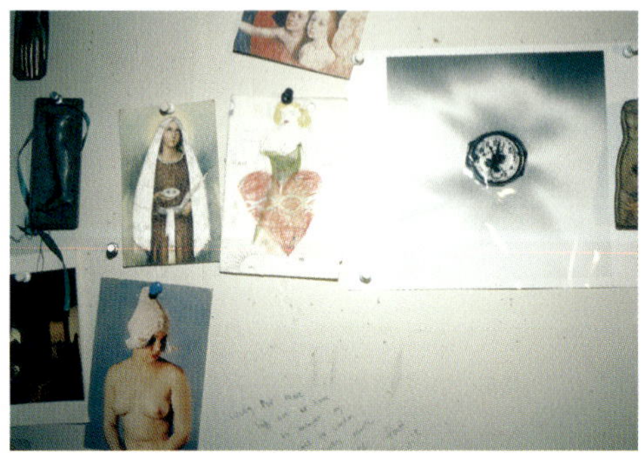

WHAT I THOUGHT WAS MY FREEDOM,
BECAME MY PRISON.

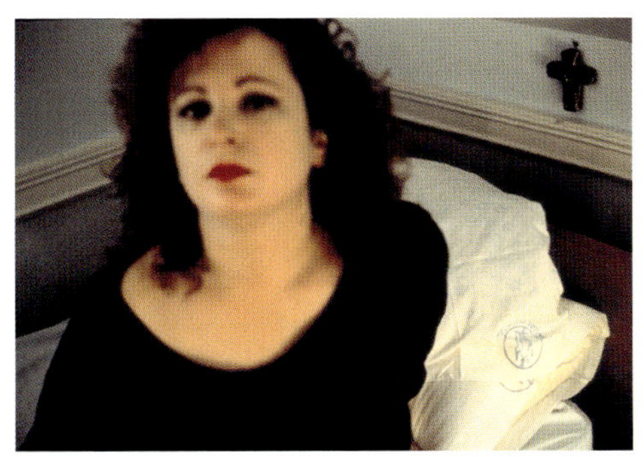

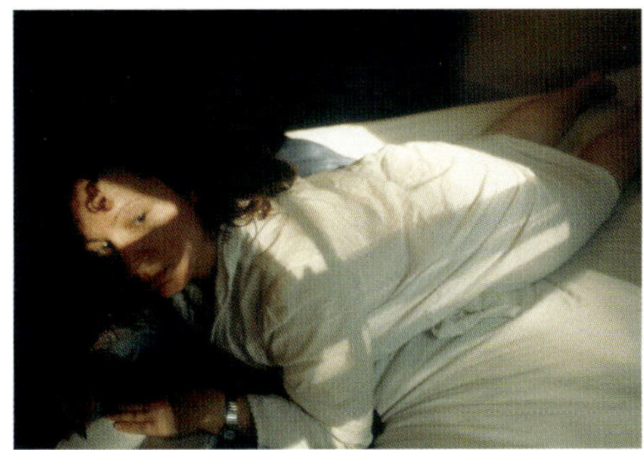

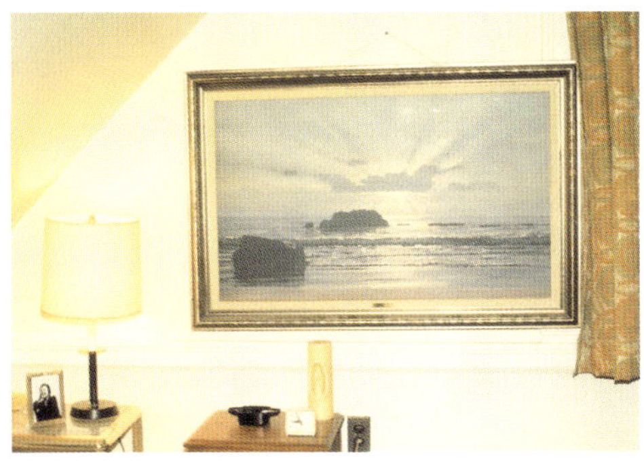

During my first recovery from drugs
I discovered daylight.

I STAYED CLEAN FROM DRUGS
AND ALCOHOL FOR SIX YEARS.
THEN, AFTER AN OPERATION,
I BEGAN TO RELAPSE.

SELF-PORTRAIT ON THE TRAIN
BOSTON-NEW HAVEN, 1997

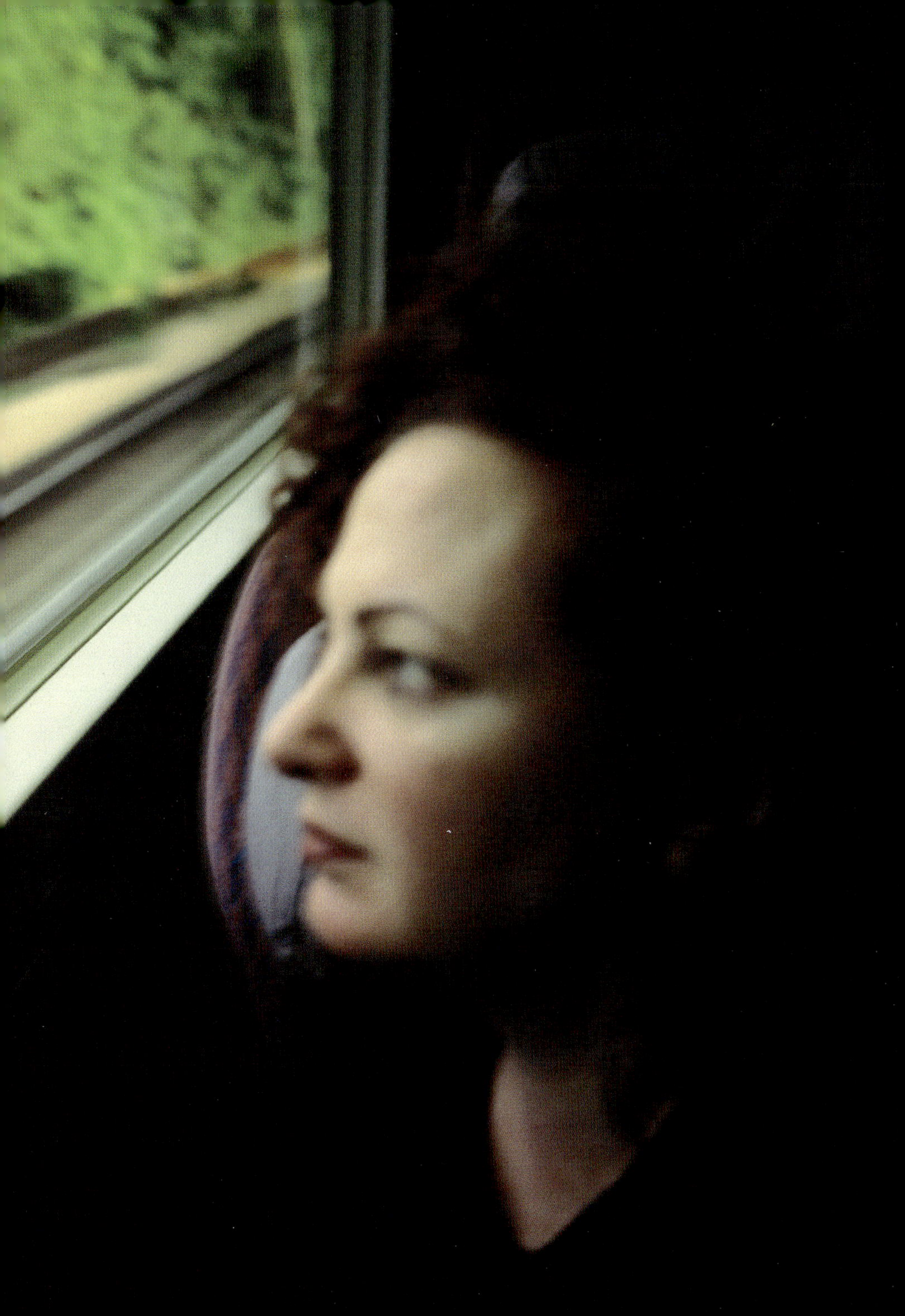

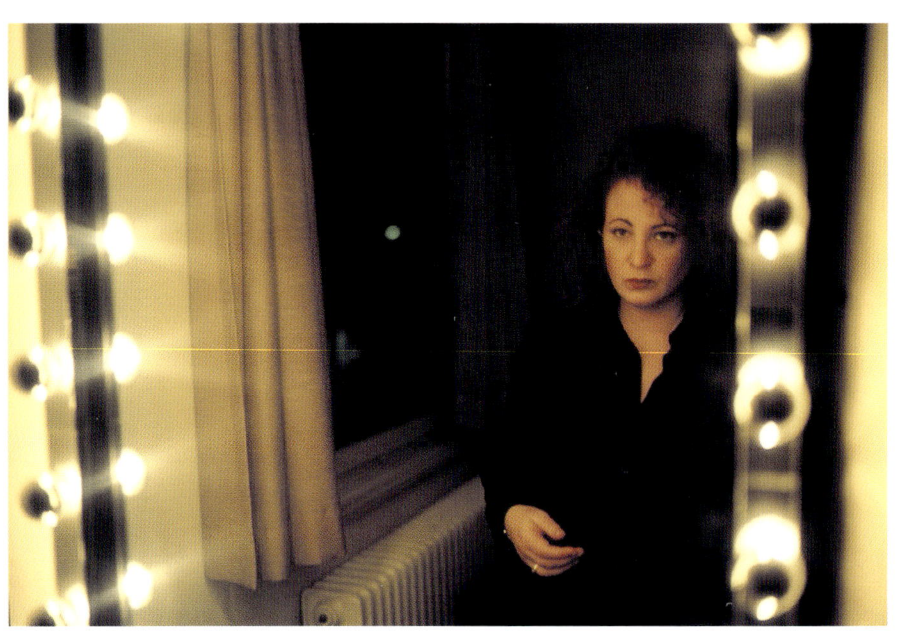

Self-portrait, Baur au Lac Hotel, Zurich, 1998

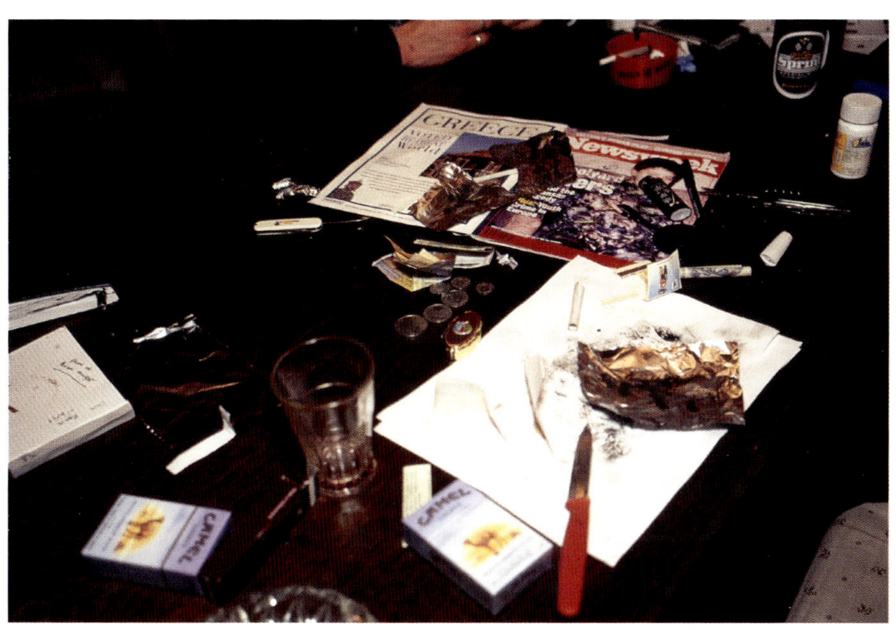

Drugs on the table, Jungfrau, Switzerland, 1998

Next page: Self-portrait on the bridge,
Golden River, Silver Hill Hospital, Connecticut, 1998

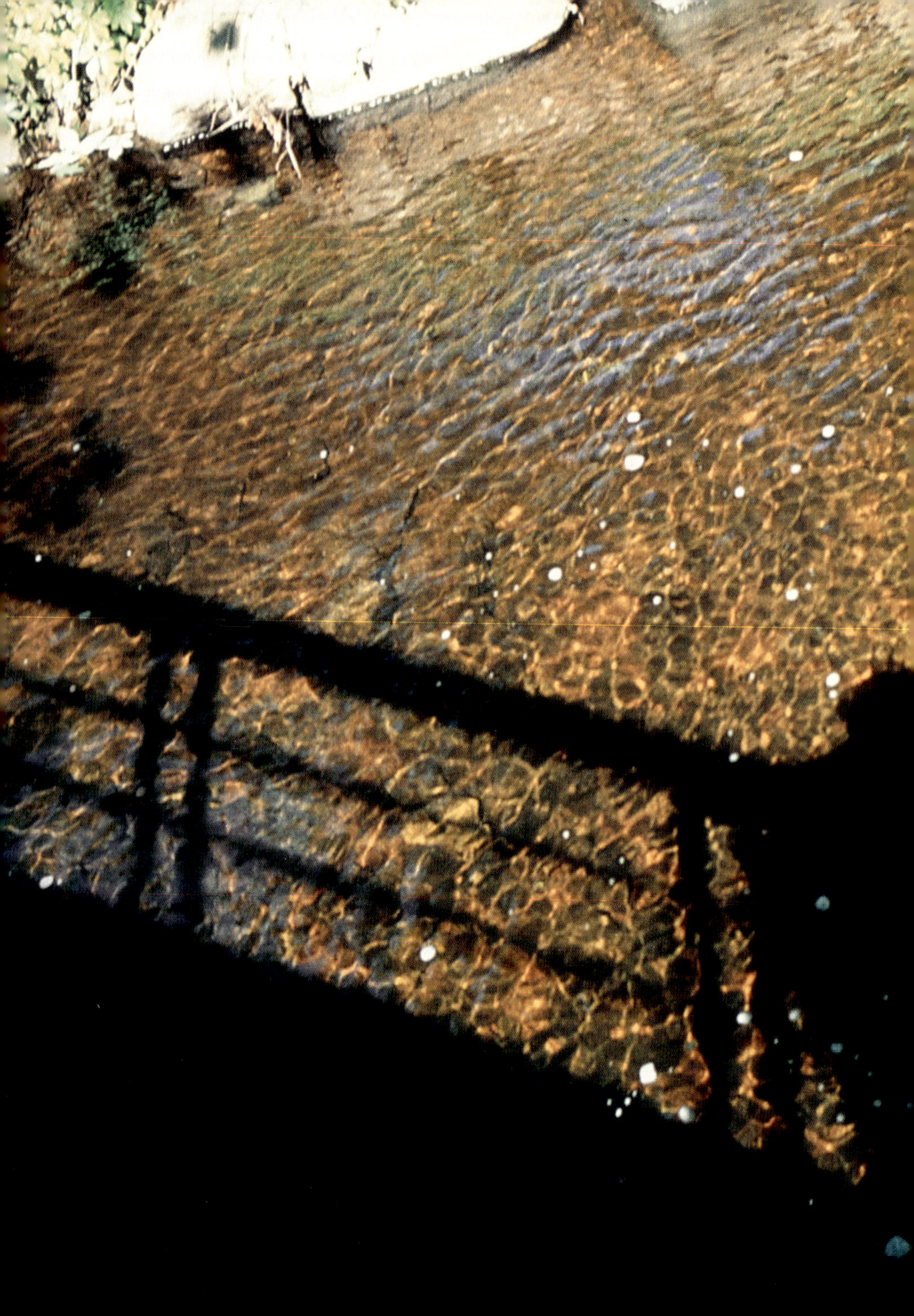

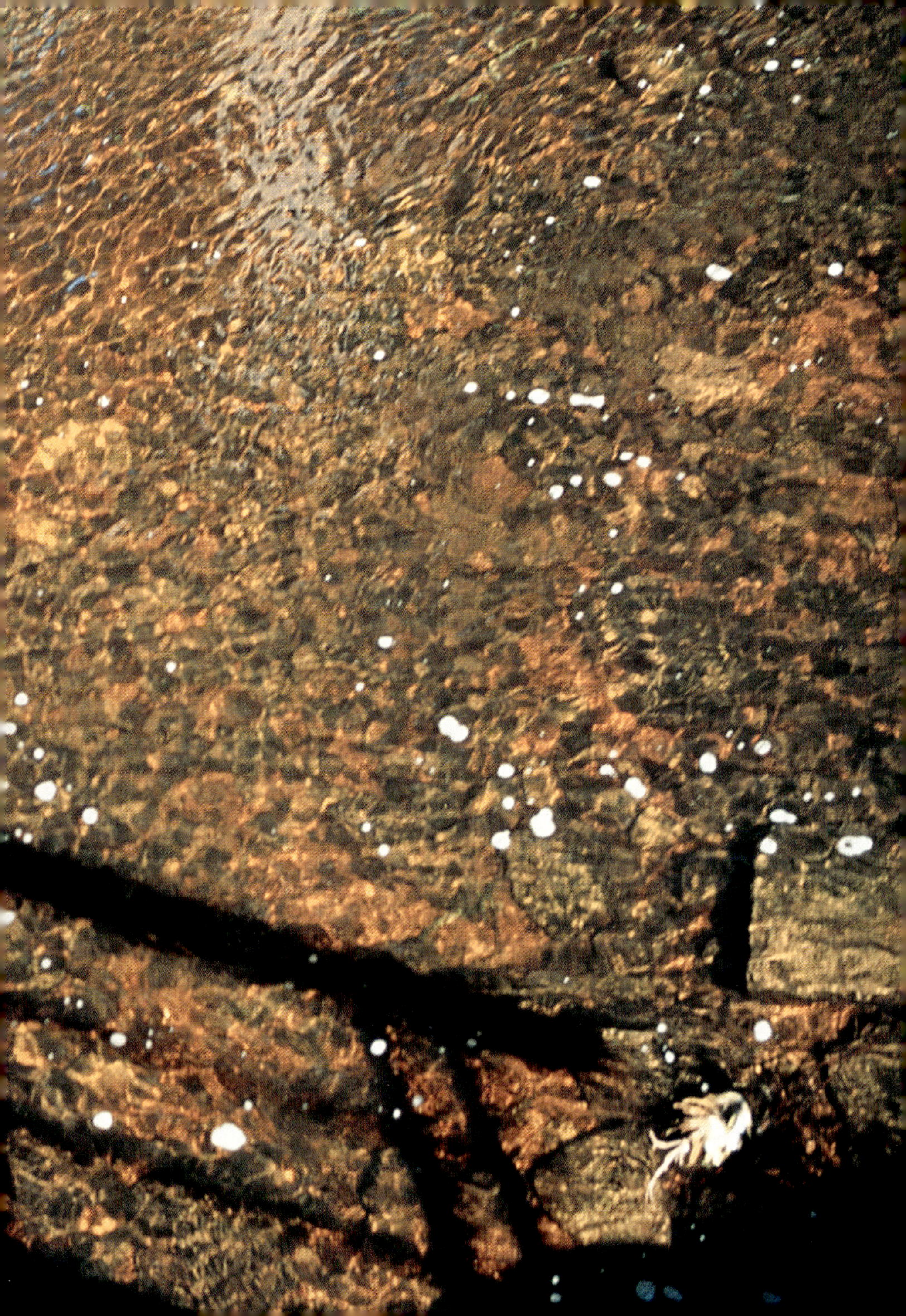

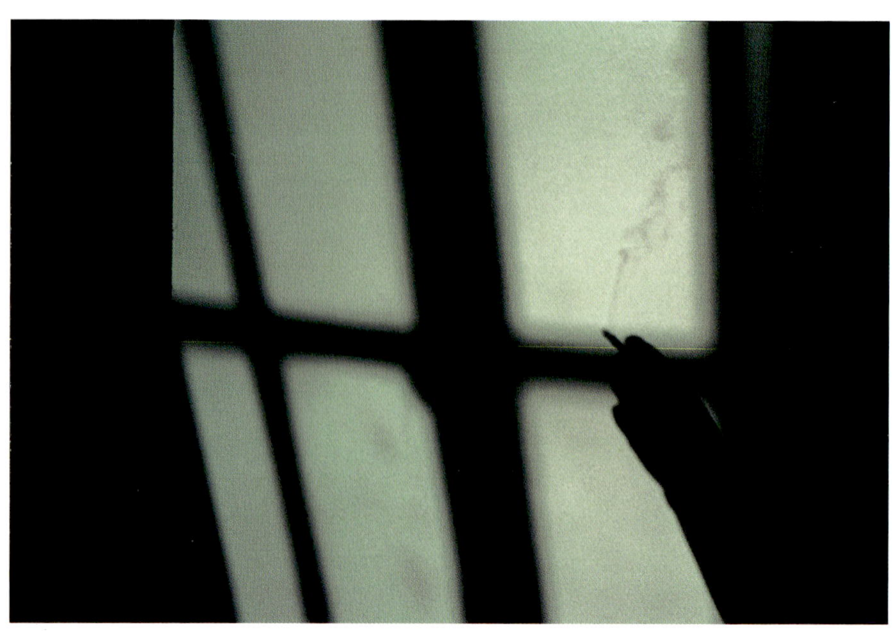

Smoking in my room, The Priory Hospital, London, 2002

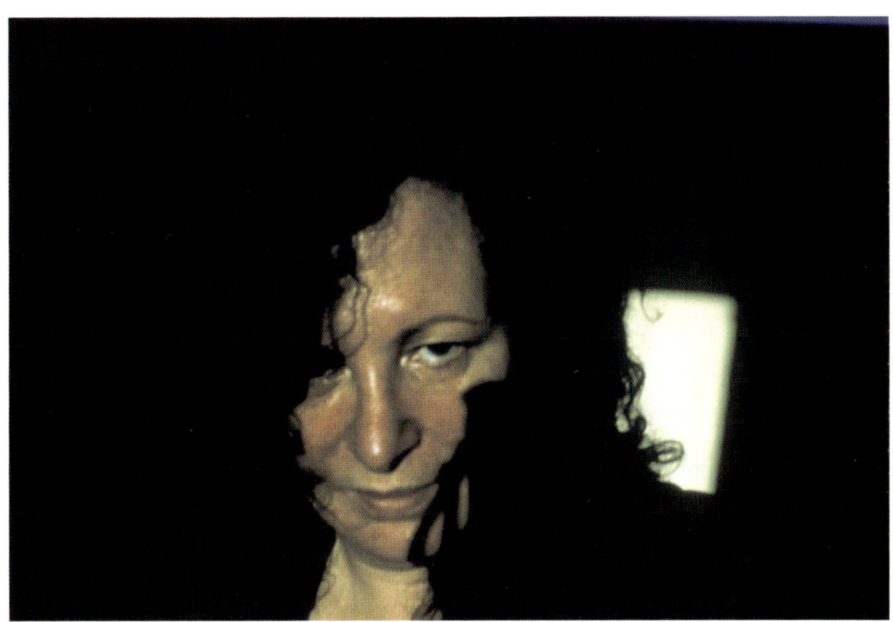

Self-portrait in delirium, The Priory Hospital, London, 2002

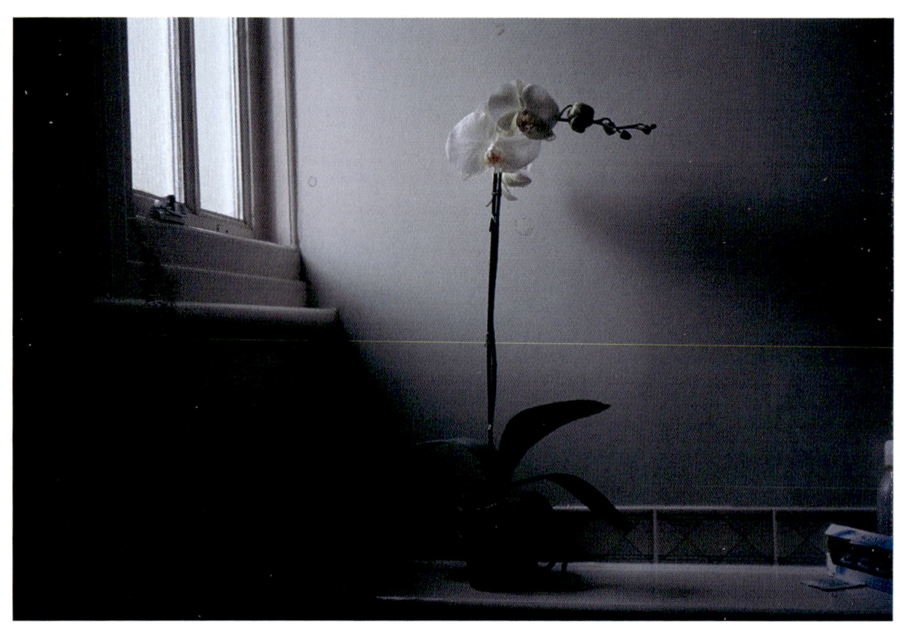

Orchid in my bathroom, The Priory Hospital, London, 2002

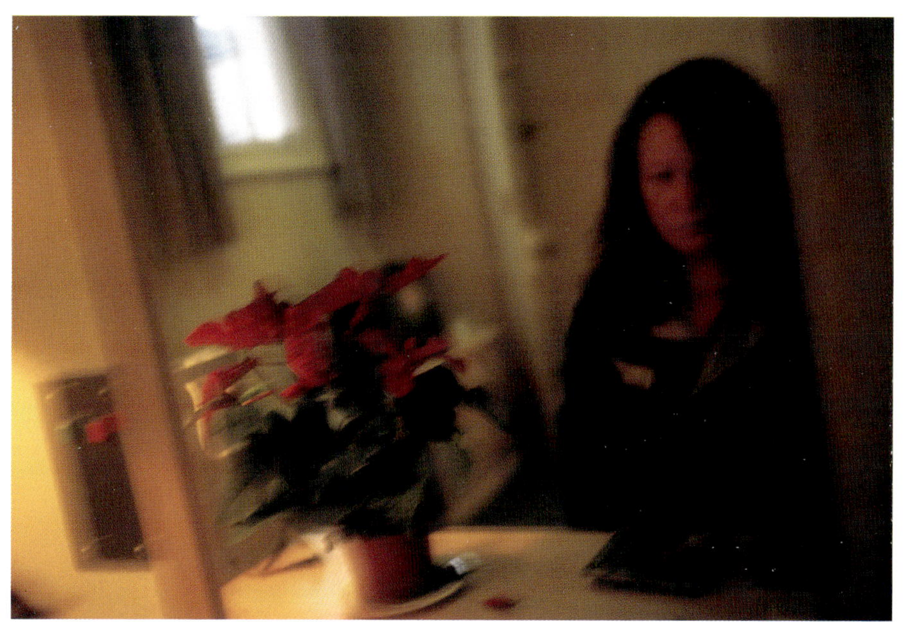

Self-portrait in pyjamas, The Priory Hospital, London, 2002

Next page: The Priory Hospital distorted in reflection, London, 2002

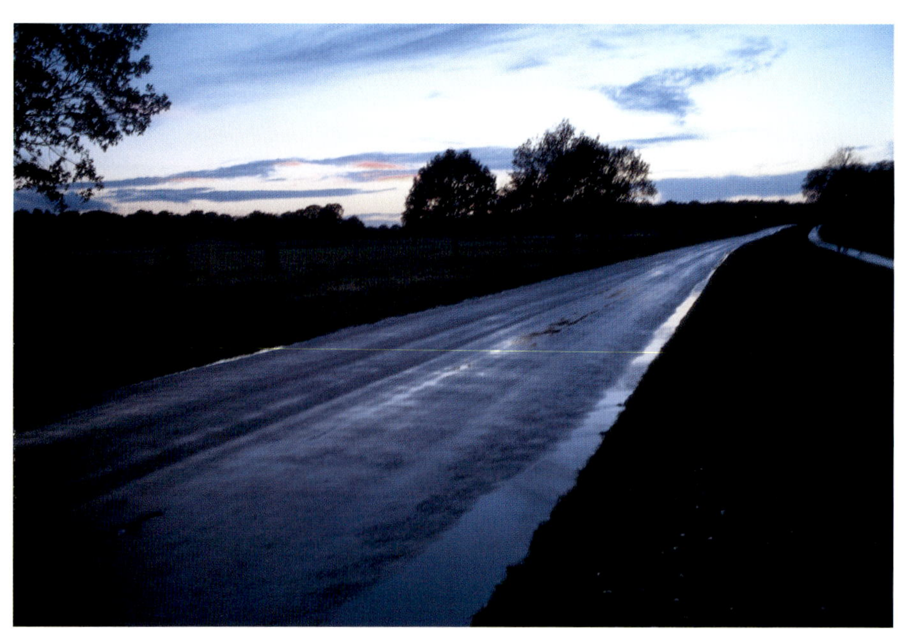

Road to the park, Roehampton, London, 2002

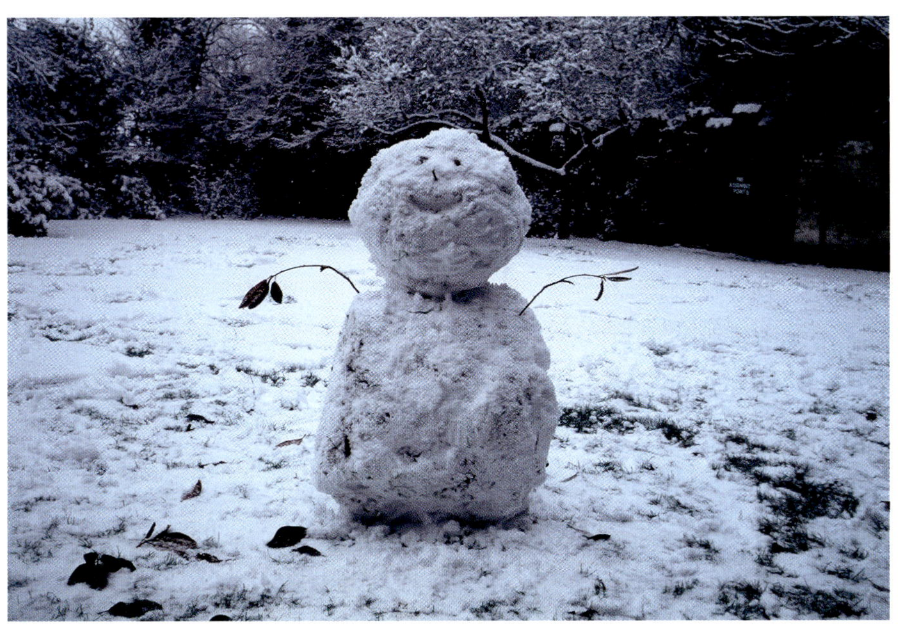

Snowman, The Priory Hospital, London, 2002

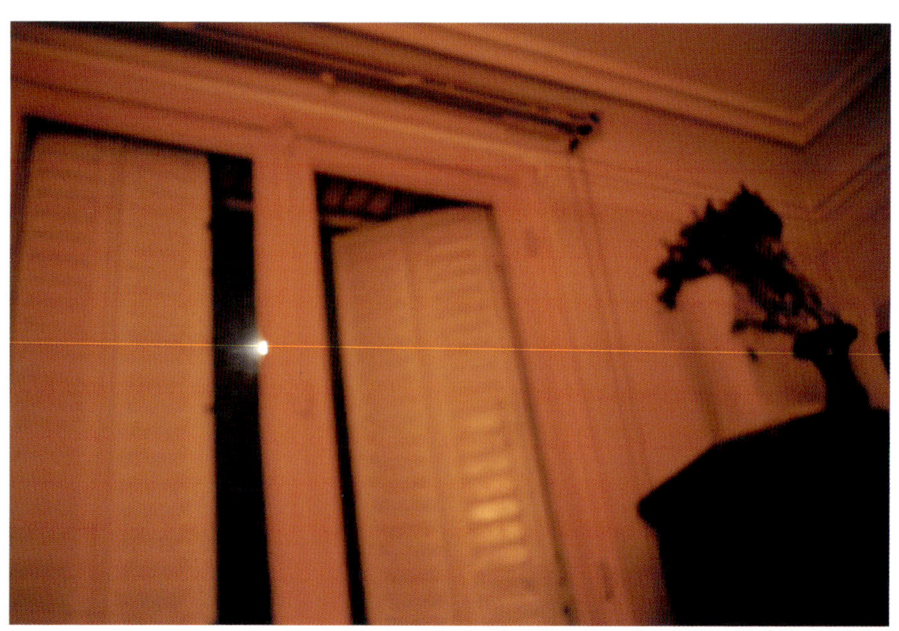

Moon in my bedroom, Paris, 2003

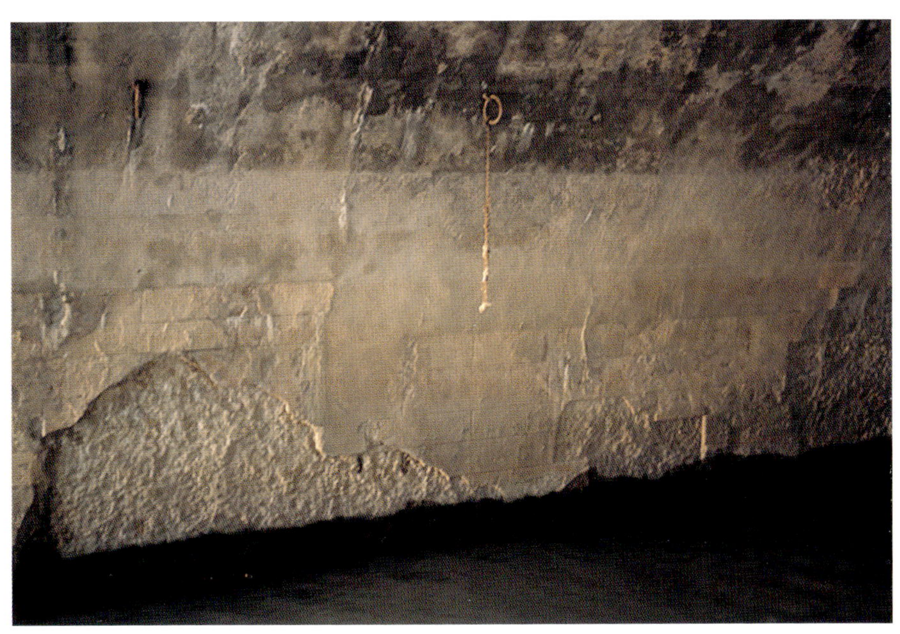

Rope under the bridge, Paris, 2003

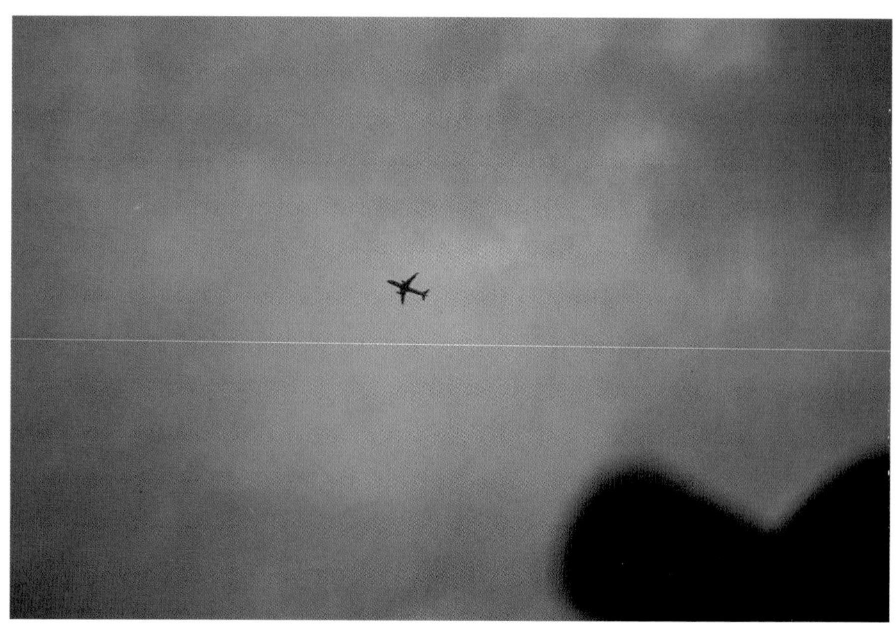

PLANE OVER THE PRIORY HOSPITAL, LONDON, 2003

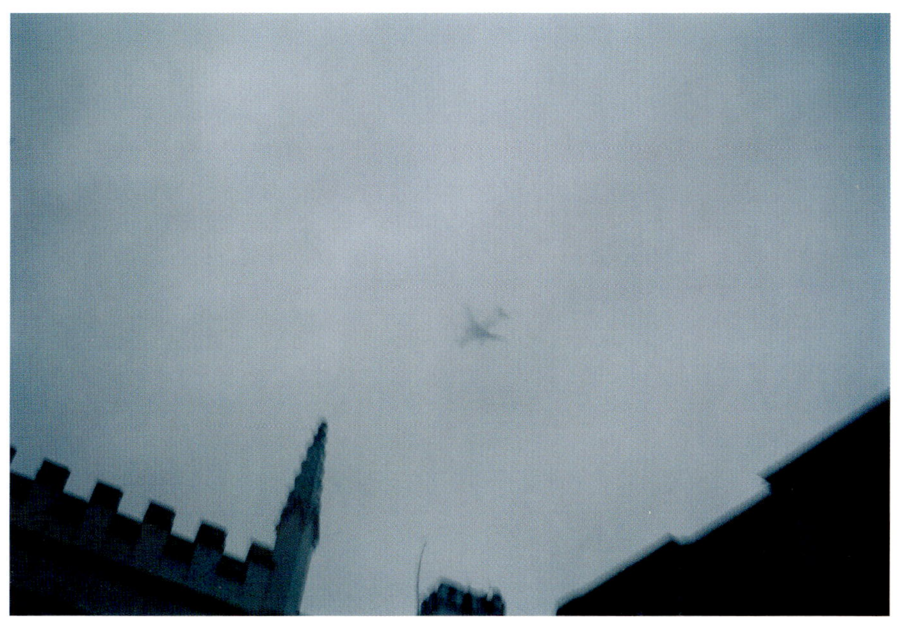

Plane disappearing, The Priory Hospital, London, 2003

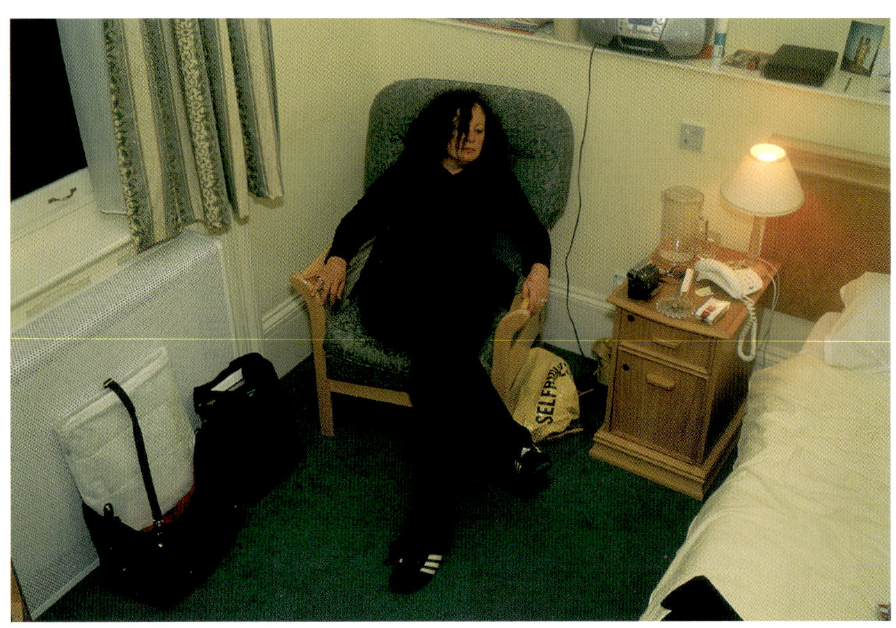

Nan in the Depression Unit, The Priory Hospital, London, 2003

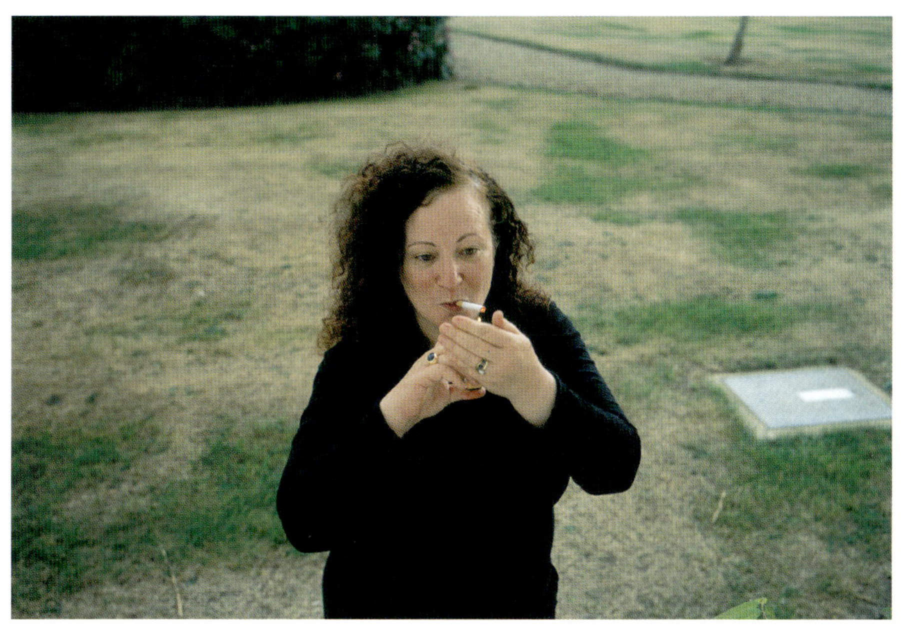

Nan during a breakdown, The Priory Hospital, London, 2003

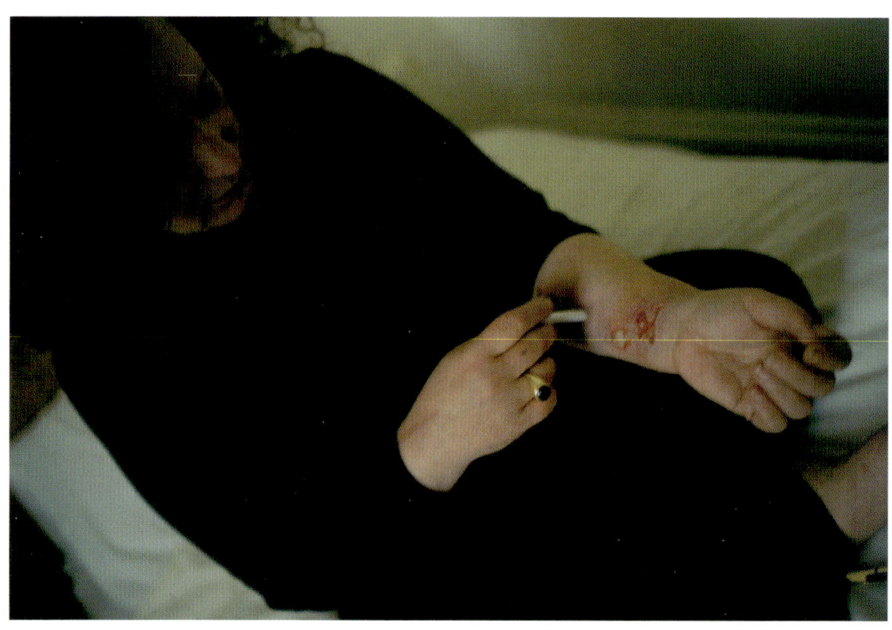

Self-mutilation, The Priory Hospital, London, 2003

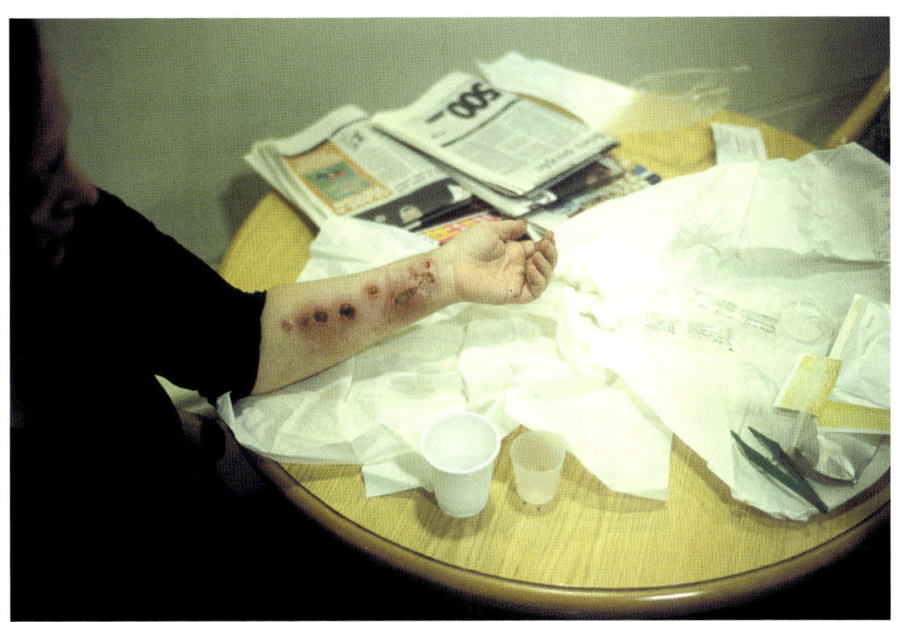

Nurses bandaging wounds, The Priory Hospital, London, 2003

"I hurt myself today to see if I still feel.
I focus on the pain the only thing that's real."

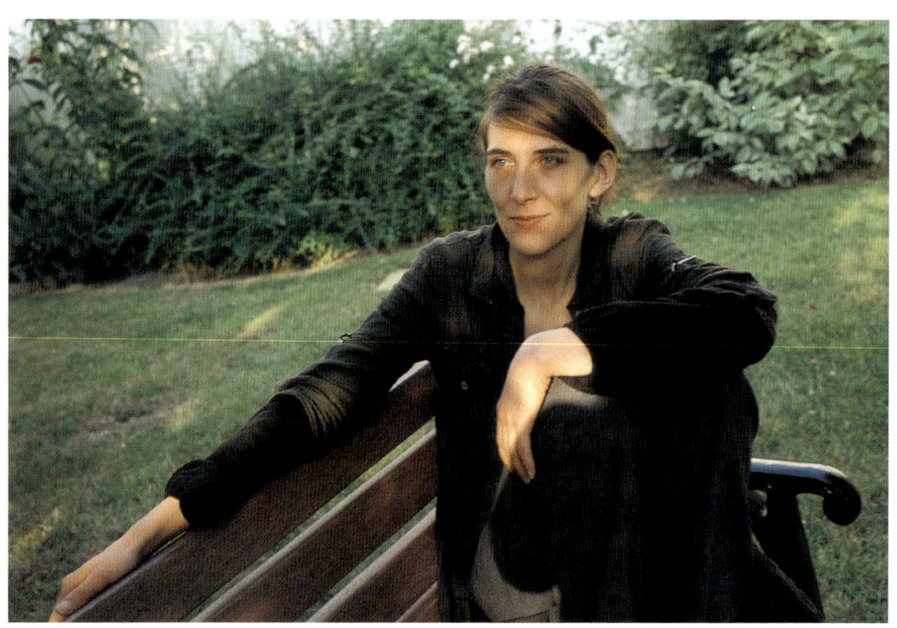

Gwen in the secret garden, The Priory Hospital, London, 2003

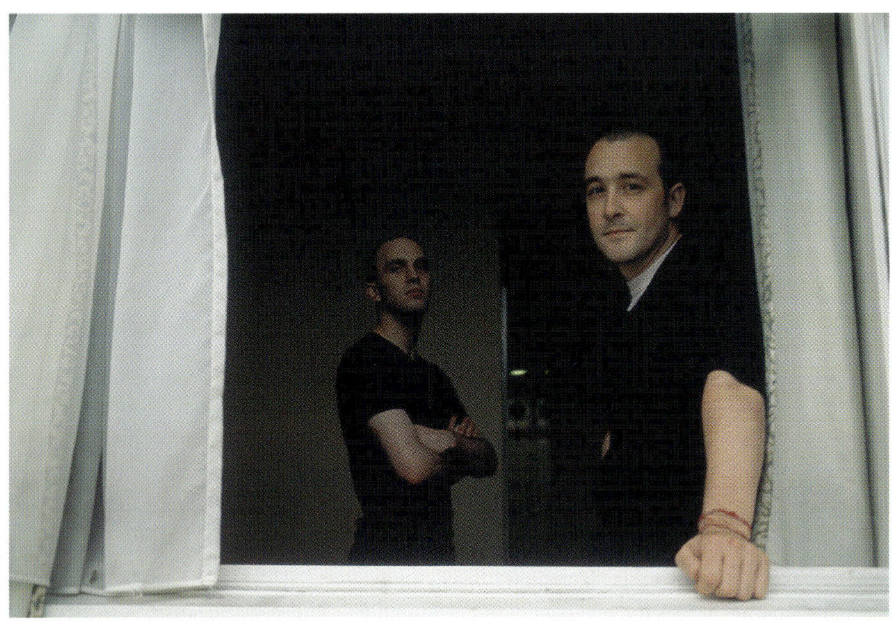

JOHN M AND JOHN J IN MY ROOM, THE PRIORY HOSPITAL, LONDON, 2003

NEXT PAGES: SUNSET LIKE HAIR, SÈTE, 2003

JABALOWE WITH PAIR OF CACTII,
HOTEL IL GABBIANO, CHIA, SARDINIA, 2003

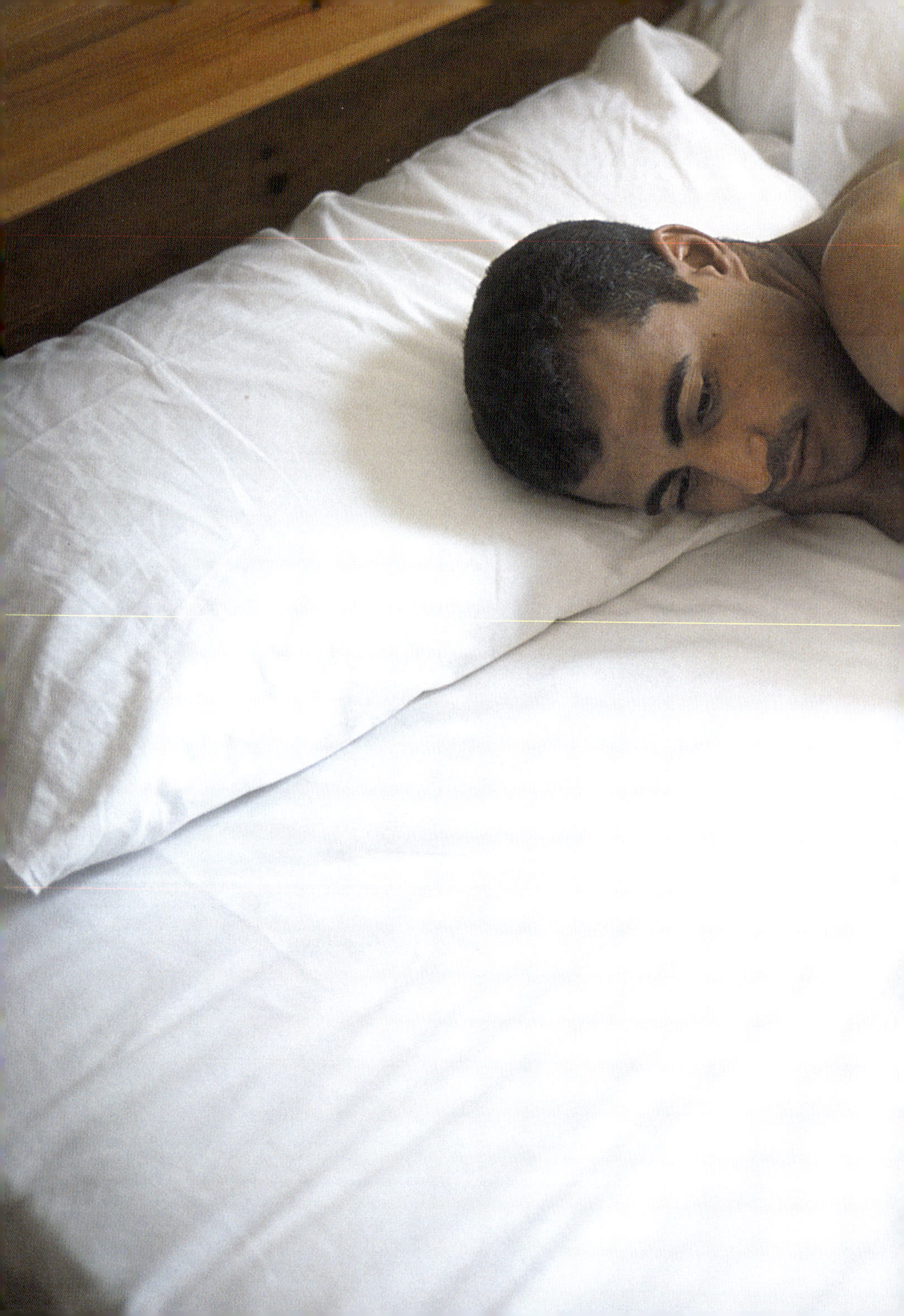

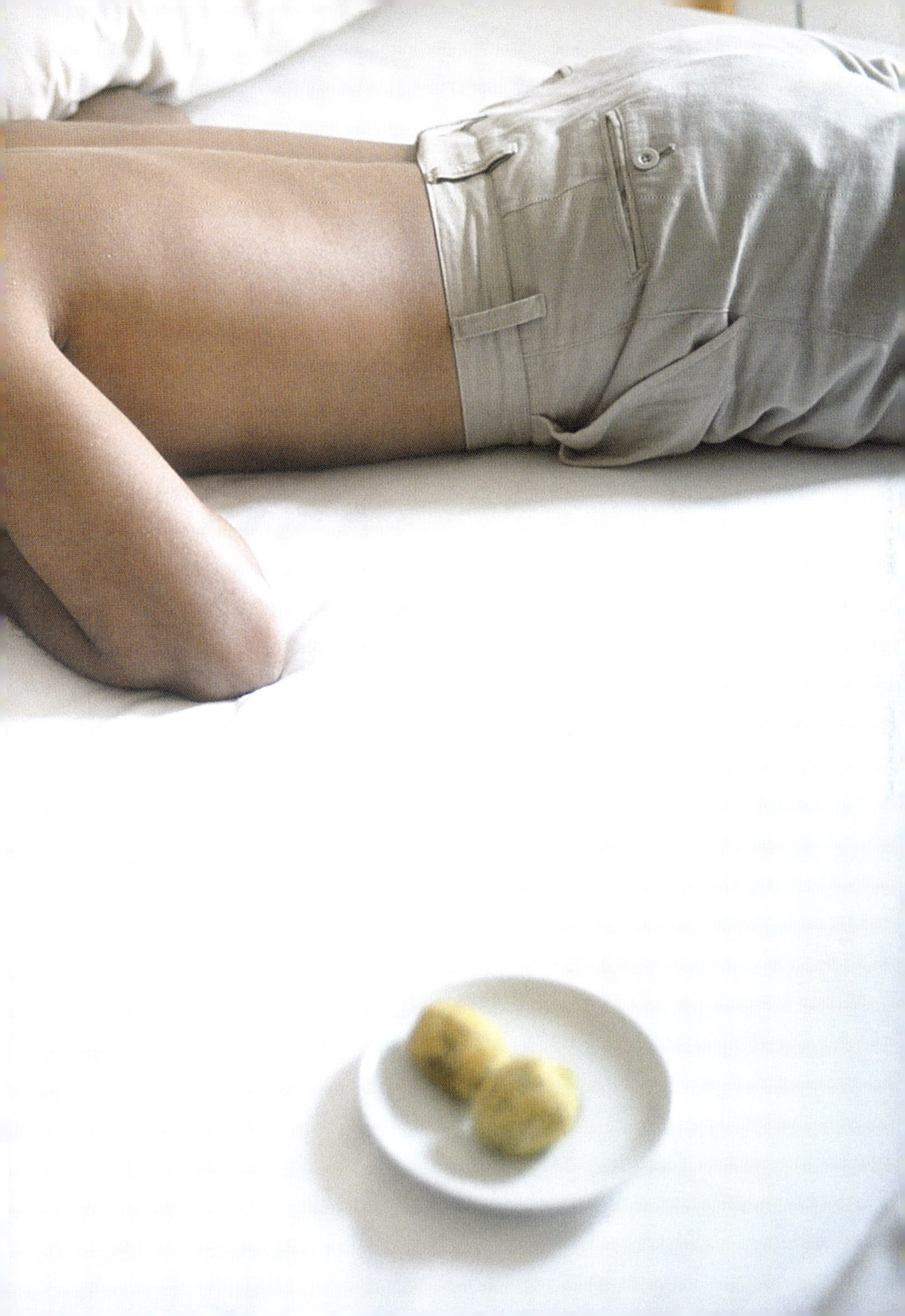

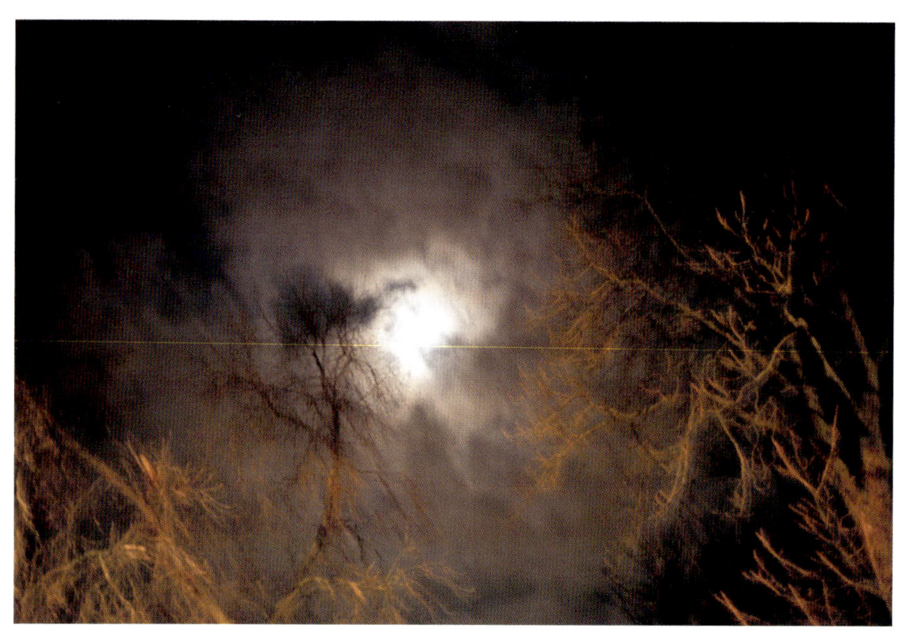

Full moon over Bois de Vincennes, Paris, 2004

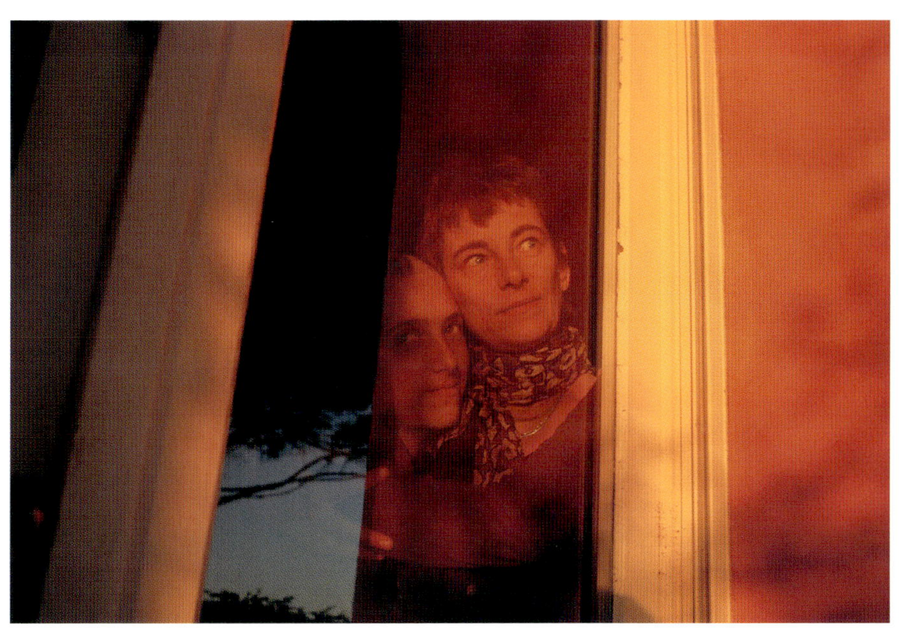

Charlotte and Marie-Anne watching sunset, Christmas Eve, Sète, 2003

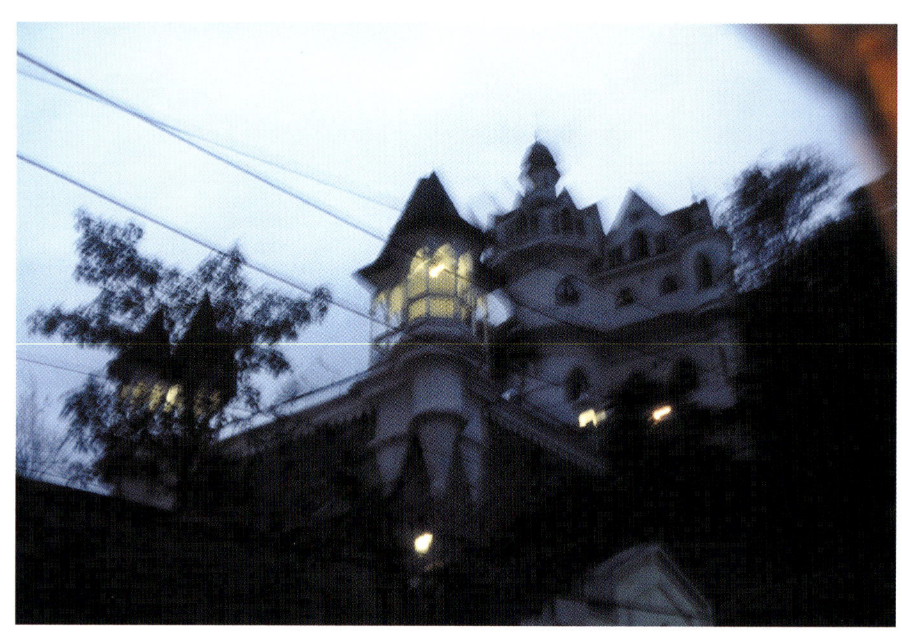

Haunted House, Santa Teresa Hill, Rio de Janeiro, Brazil, 2003

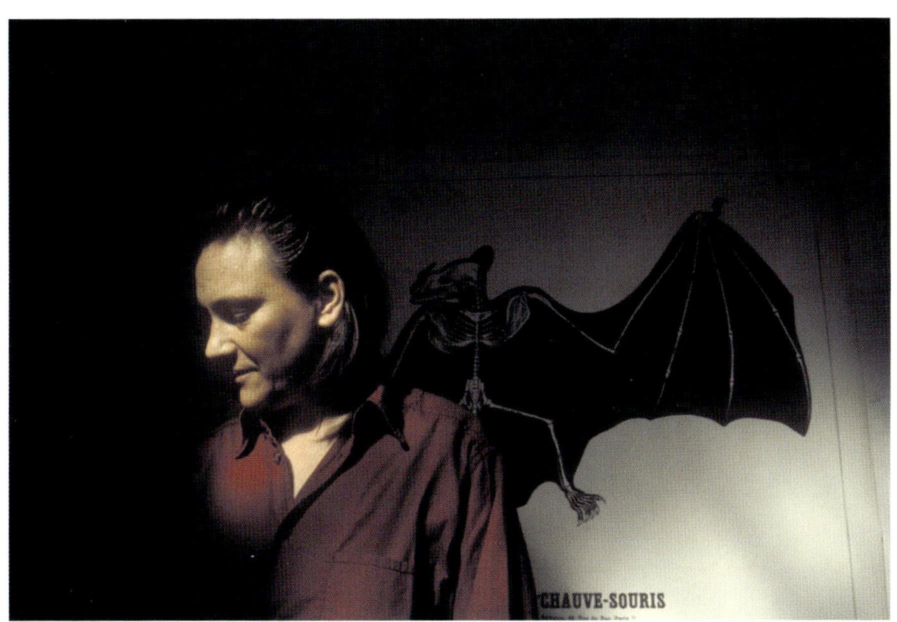

RAYMONDE IN THE EDITING STUDIO, PARIS, 2004

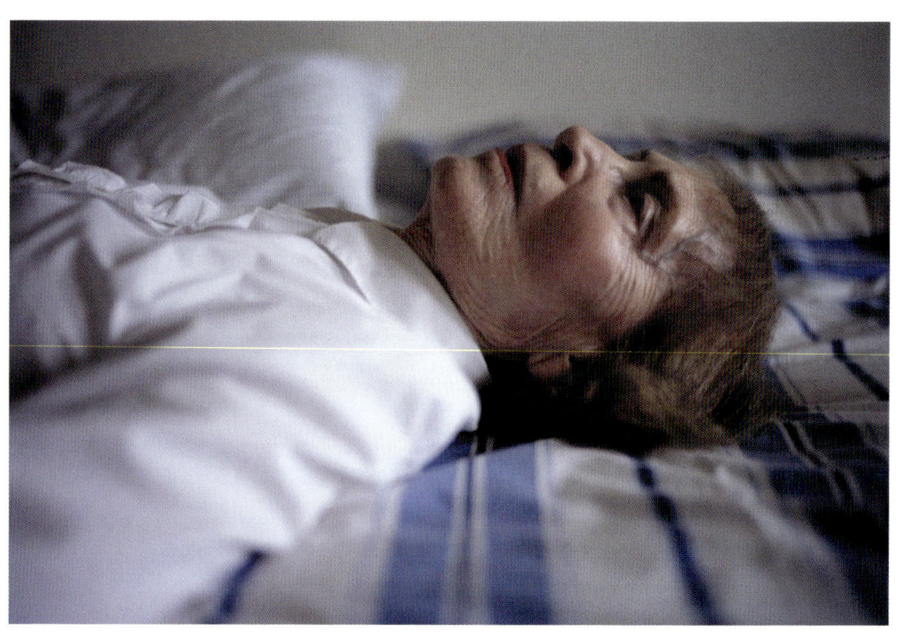

My mother laying on her bed, Salem, Massachusetts, 2004

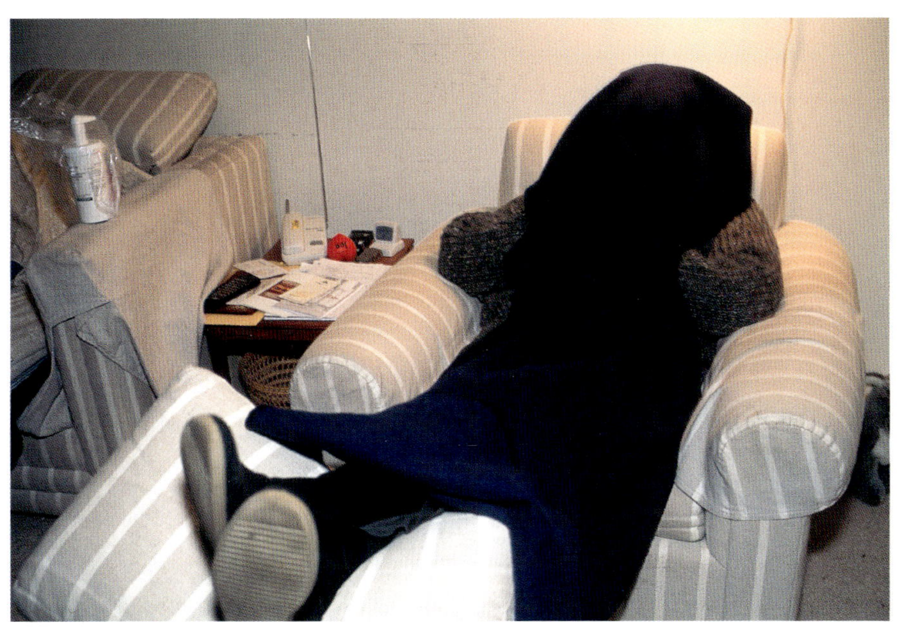

My father napping, Salem, Massachusetts, 1998

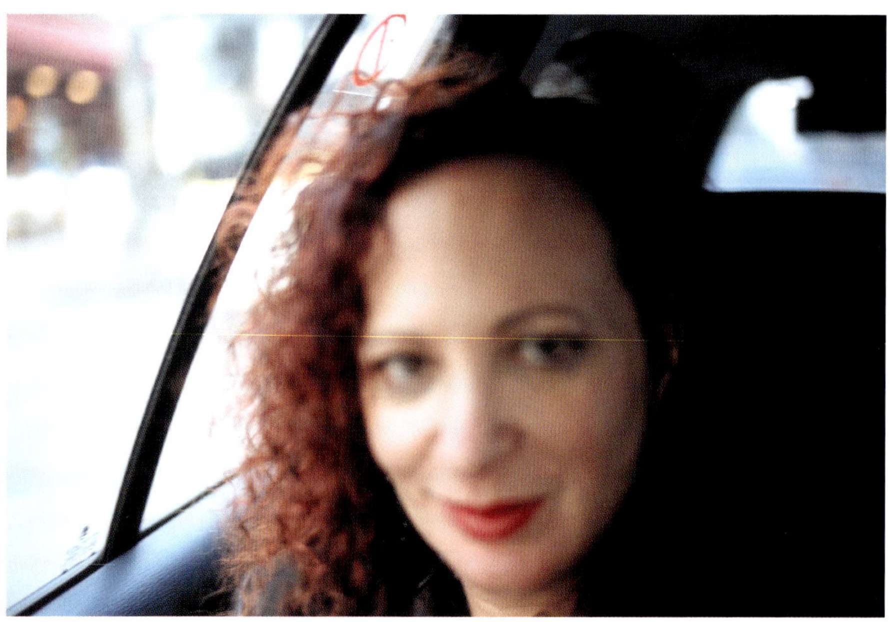

Self-portrait in a taxi, Paris, 2004

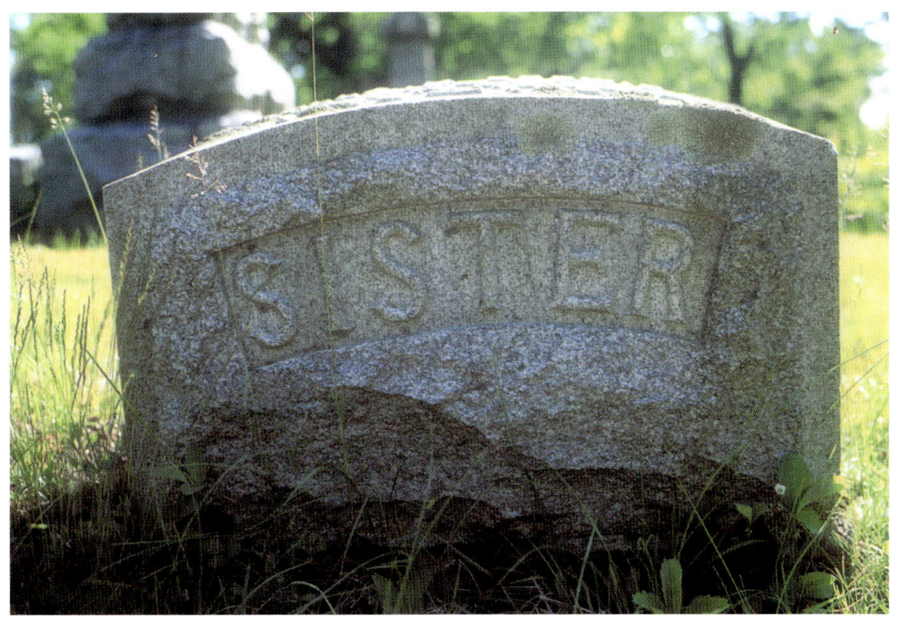

Sister grave, 2004

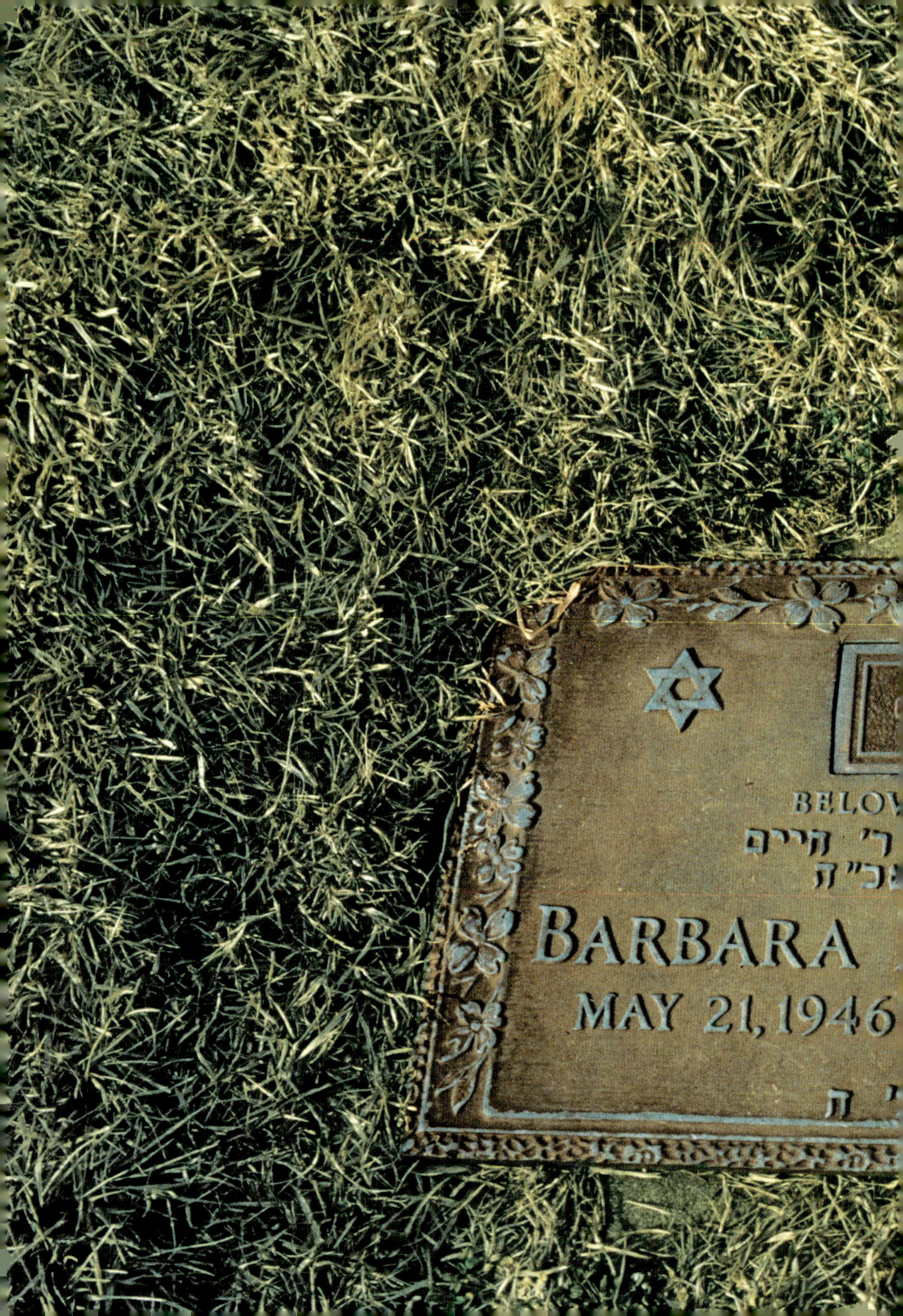
BELOV
ר' חיים
נכ"ה
BARBARA
MAY 21, 1946
ת'

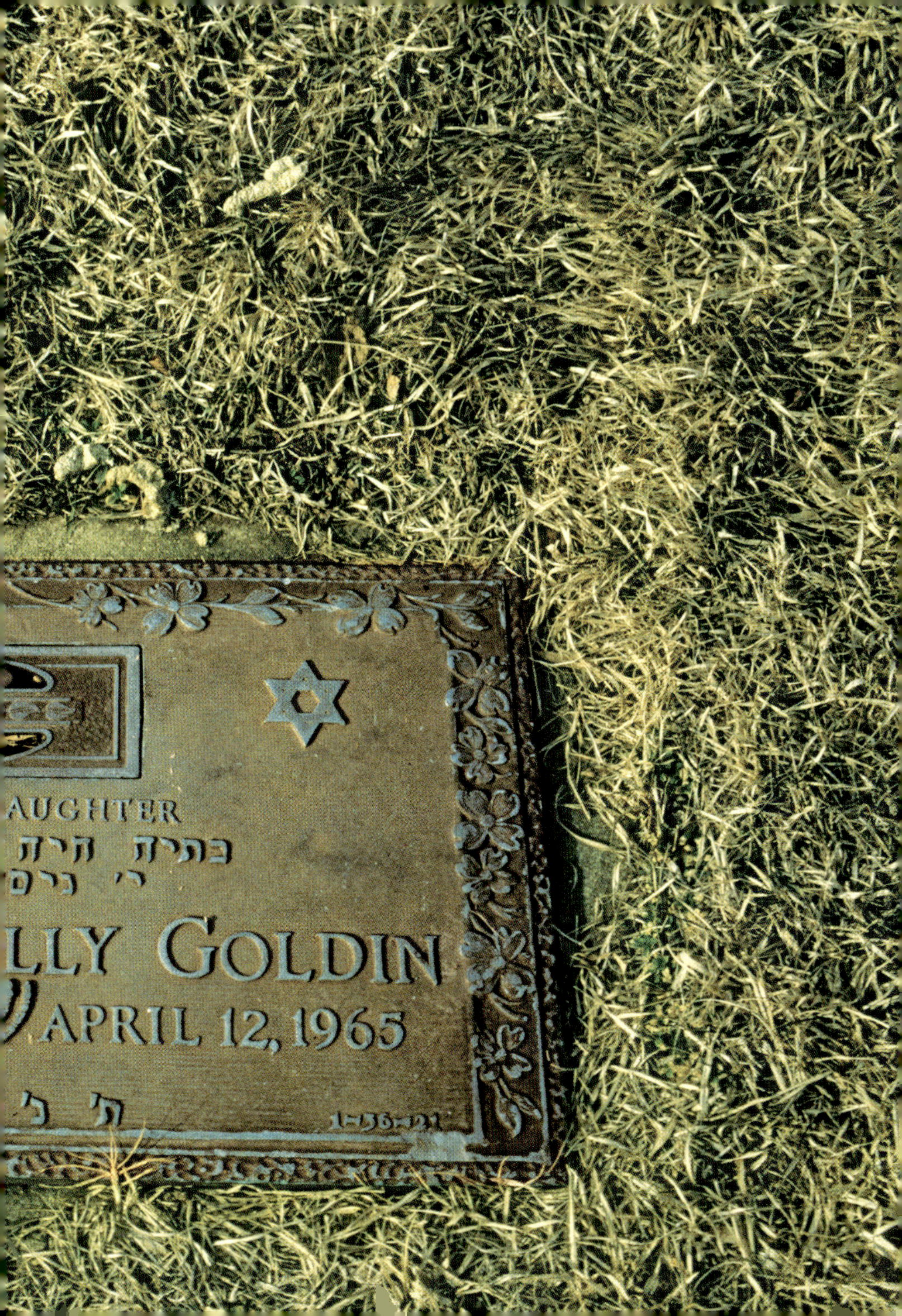
AUGHTER
בתיה חיה
י נים
LLY GOLDIN
APRIL 12, 1965
ת ל
1-56-21

How calmly she behaved that day,
bought a knife, it still had a price tag on it,
asked when the next Boston – Ohio train passed through,
found a spot, a blind curve.
I was told she lay down and waited
The death record says she lay
In front of the train
5:38 on an April afternoon
during cherry blossom season
on a day pass from a mental hospital,
some boys saw her,
tried to help her.
She threatened them with her knife.
Died of multiple injures sustained
by being dragged by the train.
And "from depression" reads the death certificate.
She was almost 19.
The conductor came the next morning.
He'd tried to stop the train.
He quit his job.

When the police came to inform us
I knew.
A Monday night, dinnertime
I'd been waiting all my conscious life for this moment
because I always believed her.
Two officers talked to my father on the lawn alone.
Then he howled, like a wounded animal
on the front lawn.
Inconsolable sound from beneath the deepest recess of the soul,
beyond any human sound I've heard since, way beyond the sound barrier
beyond language or tears, tearing the body to shreds, piercing the air.
Every suicide kills more than one person, they say.
My mother said to the police:
"Tell the children it was an accident"
Who was she trying to protect?
That was my moment of clarity that defined my life,
my break with the family, I was 11.
The tyranny of revisionism even at the moment of greatest anguish.
Suburbia. Don't let the neighbors know. Or even the children.
Rewrite history immediately before it can be written.

N.G. 2004

Next pages

S.S.S., installation at Chapelle de La Salpêtrière, Paris, September 2004:
First spread: Set of clinic. Second spread: Wax figure of girl
in hospital being restrained. Third spread: Man hit by lightning.

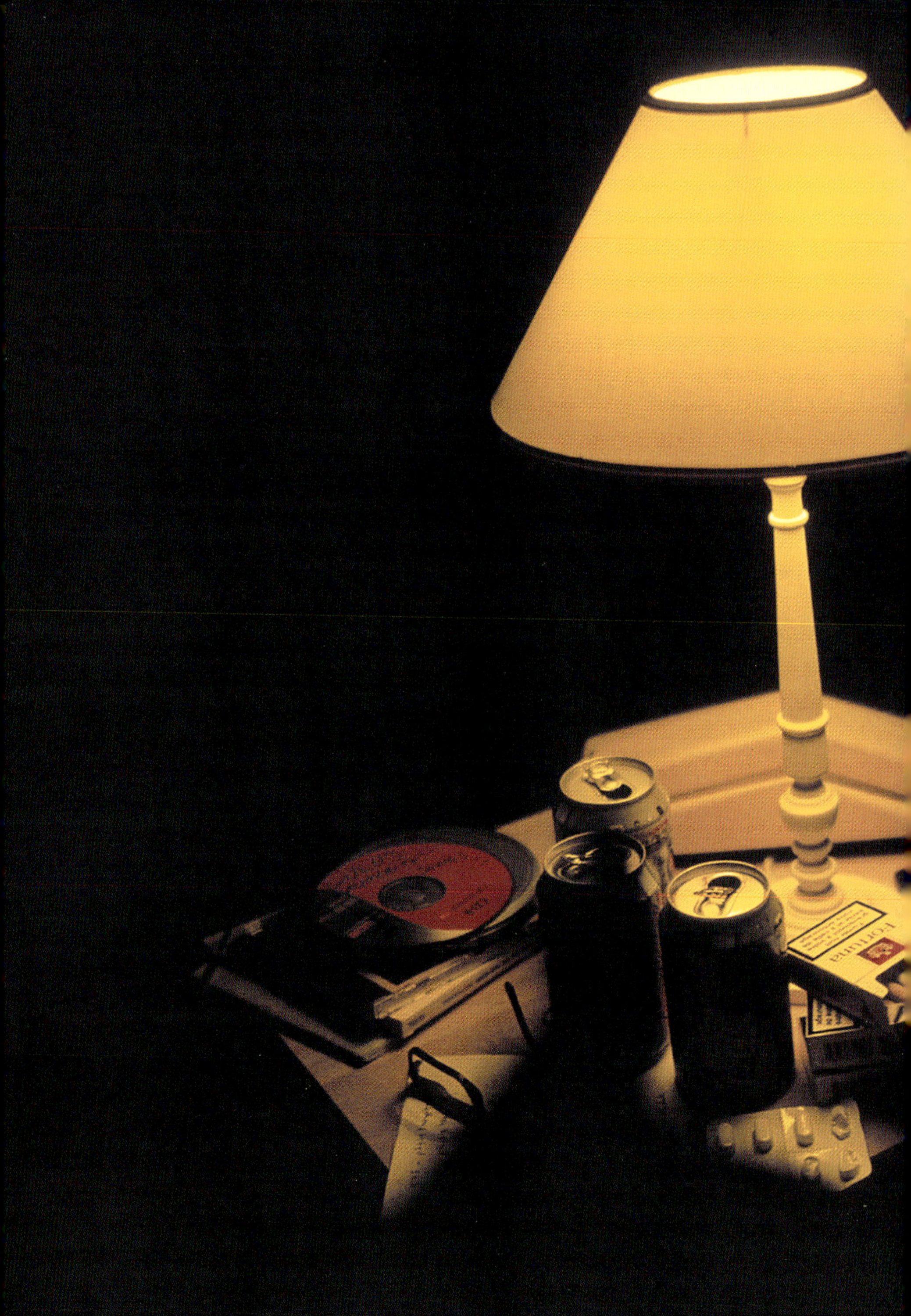

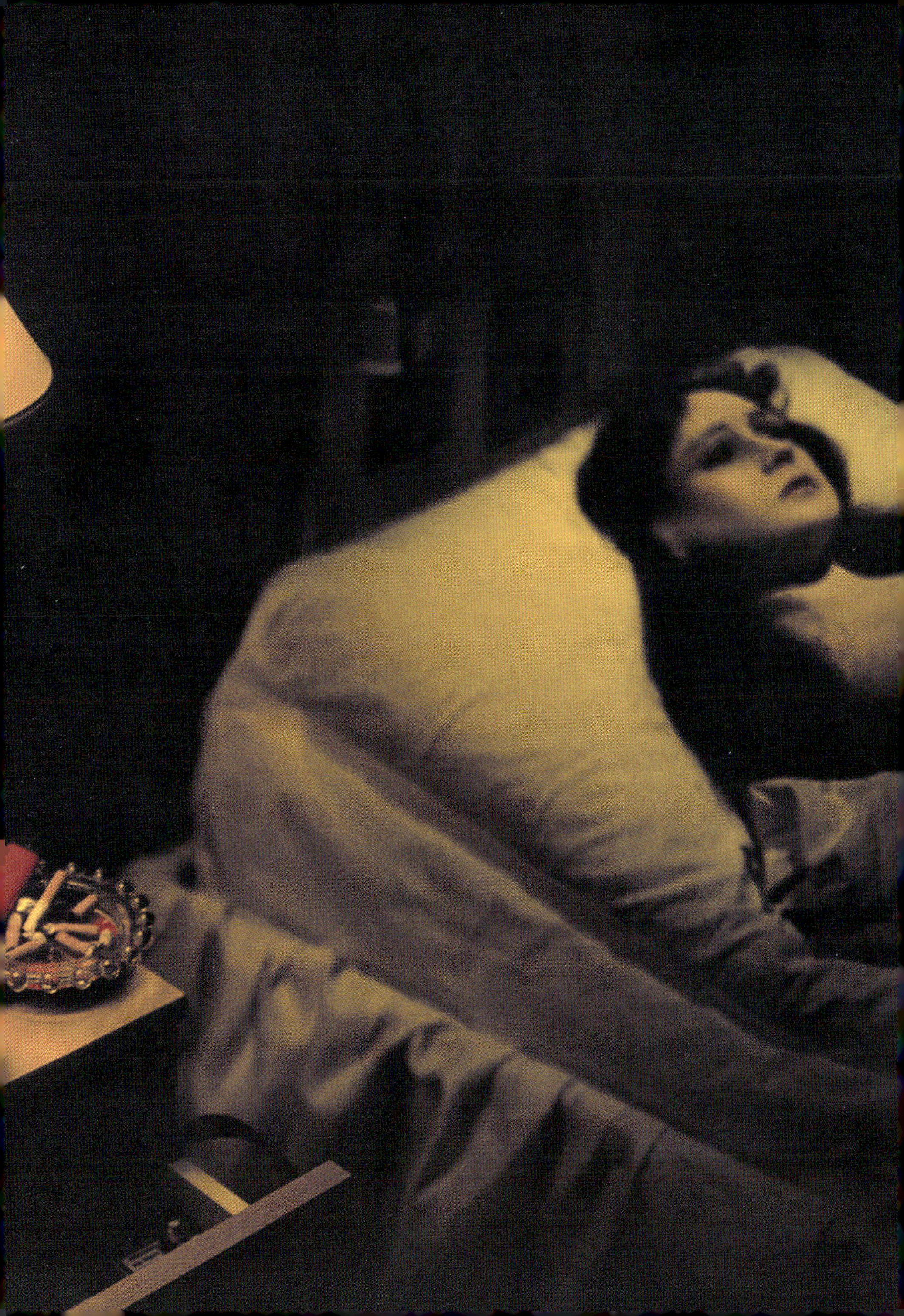

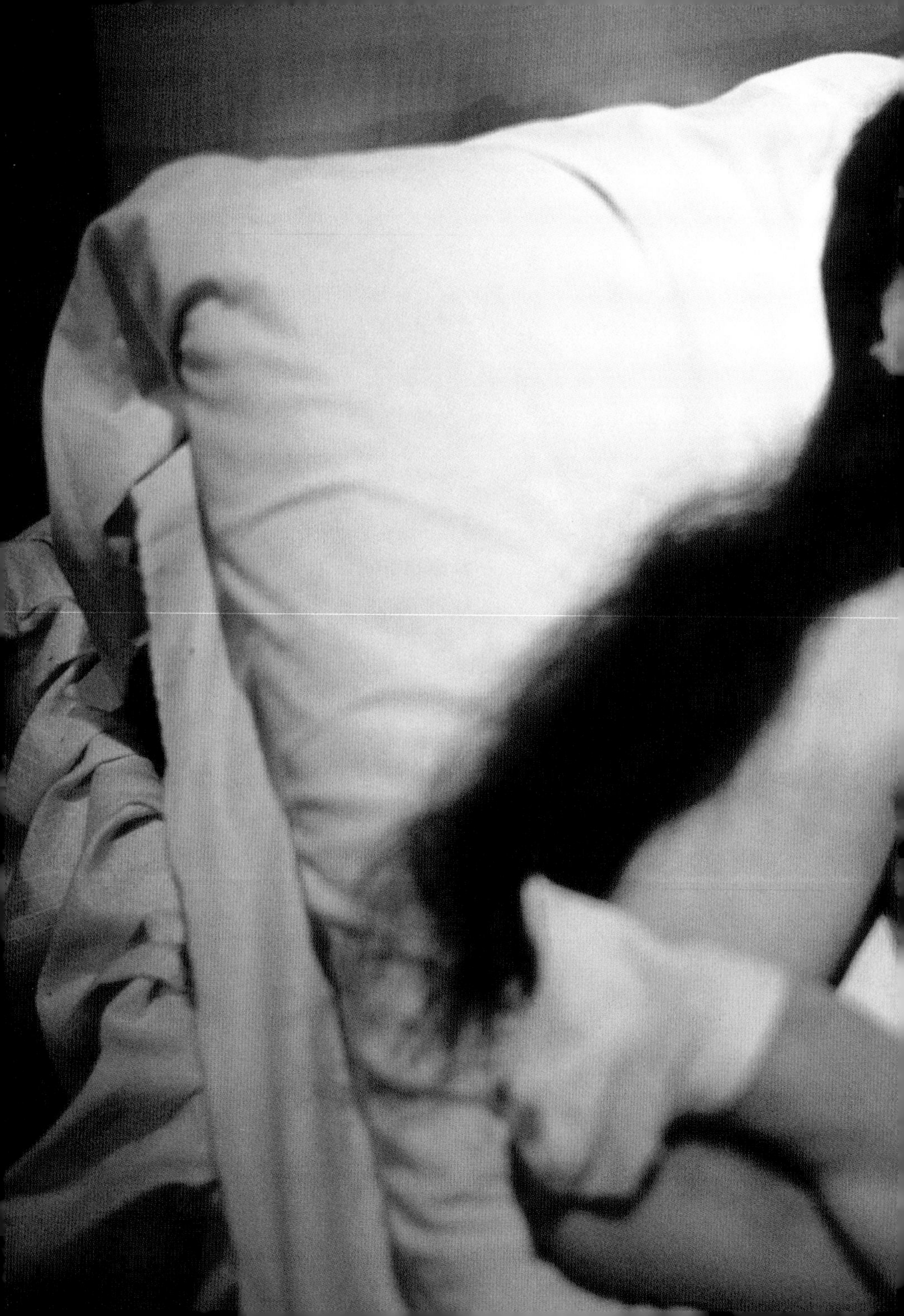

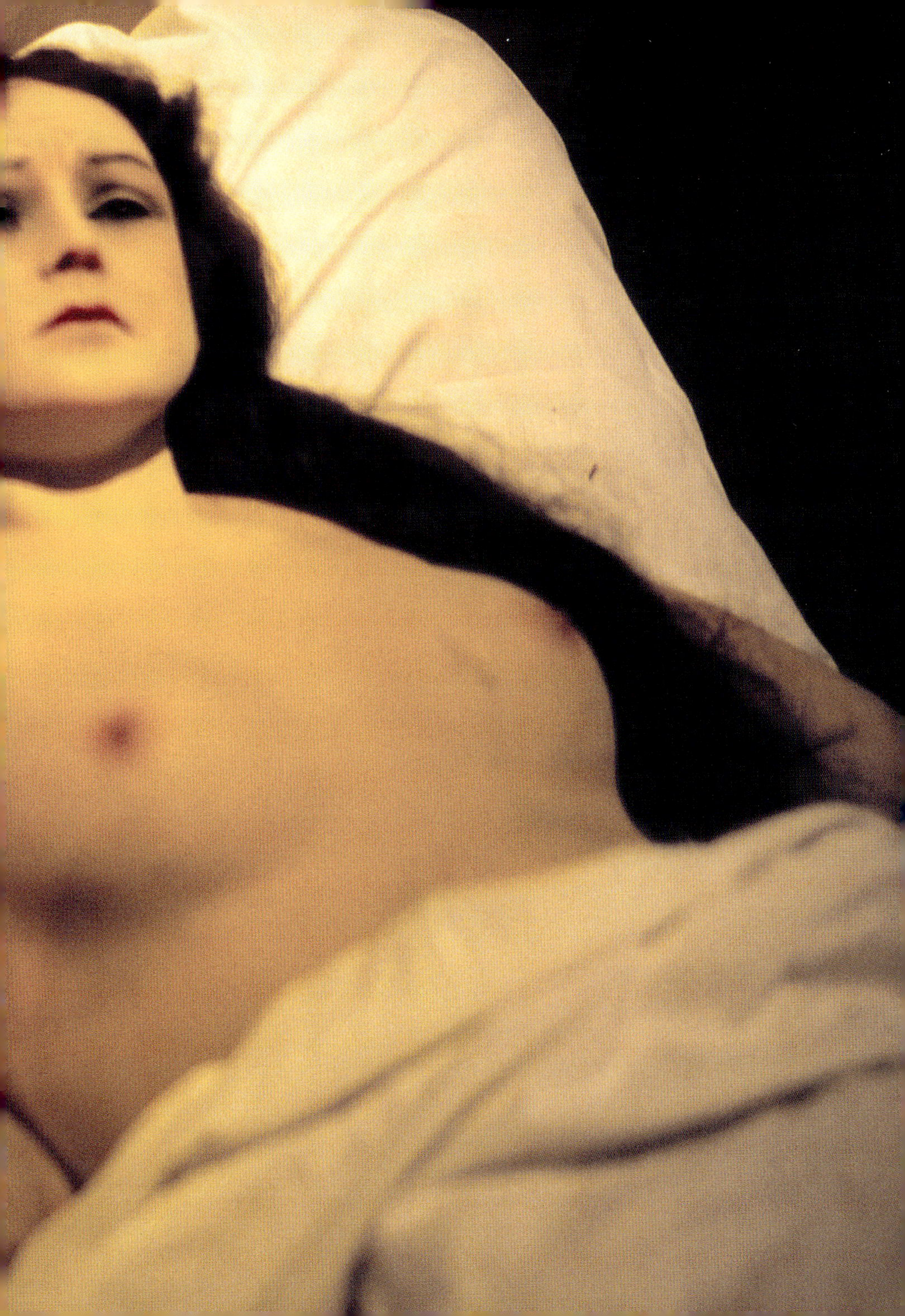

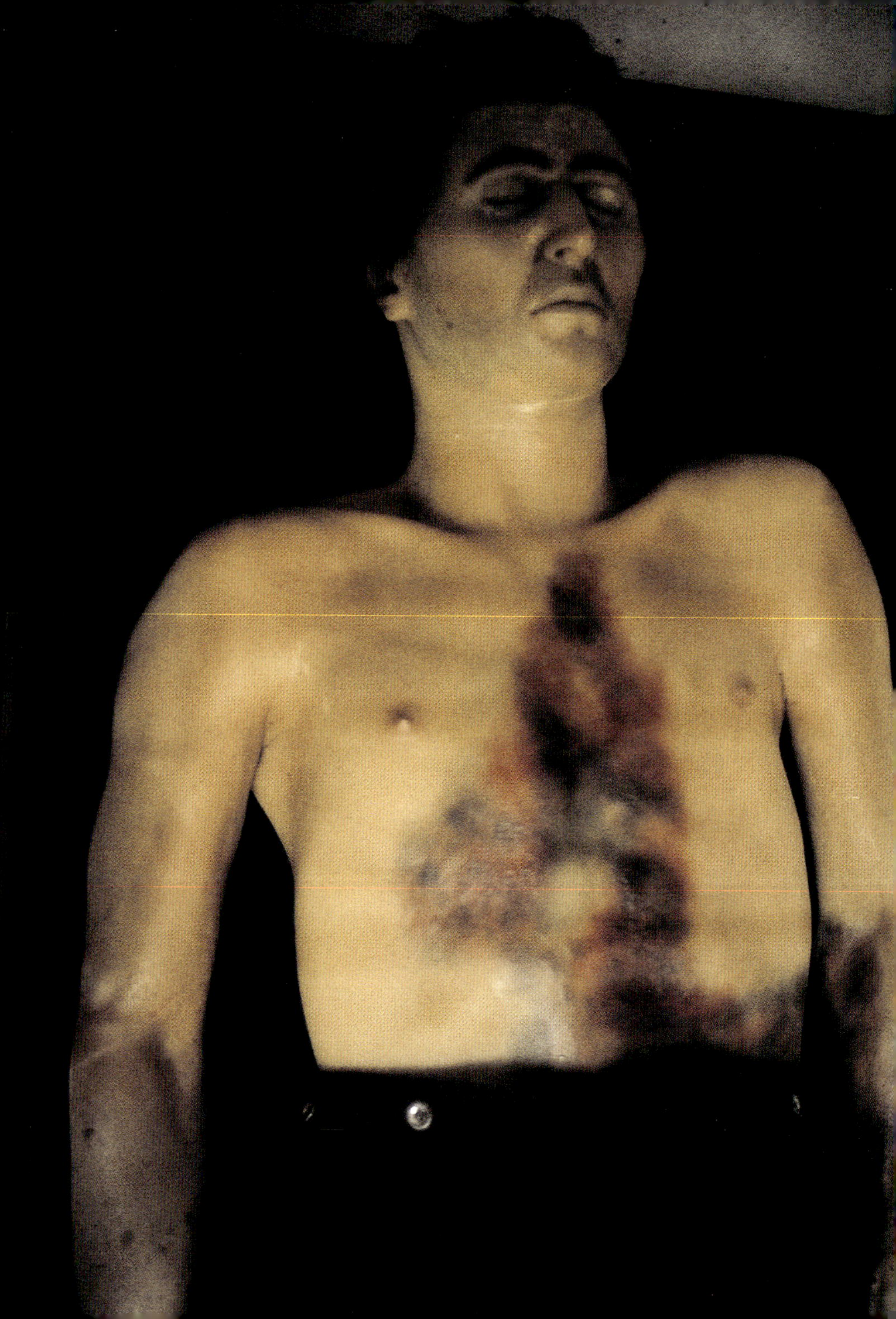

ALWAYS AND ABOVE ALL
FOR MY BELOVED SISTER: BARBARA HOLLY GOLDIN
1946–1965

THANKS TO MY COLLABORATORS WITHOUT WHOM
SISTERS, SAINTS, AND SIBYLS WOULD NOT EXIST
RAYMOND COUVREU
ERWAN HUON

TO MY PRECIOUS PARENTS: MY FATHER HYMAN GOLDIN AND
MY BEAUTIFUL MOTHER LILLIAN, WHO HAVE STRUGGLED
BRAVELY TO SURVIVE FOR 90 YEARS

SPECIAL THANKS 2026:
ALEX KWARTLER
ZOE FREILICH

FOR BRINGING THE INSTALLATION TO LIFE:
ALEX KWARTLER
HALA WARDÉ
MARK DAVIS
FREDRIK LIEW
KRZYSZTOF MIEKUS
FABIAN GAWLIK
MICHAEL WADE

SPECIAL THANKS 2004:
ALAIN CROMBECQUE
JOHN MARCHANT
MARIE COLLIN
NICOLAS PAGES
GWÉNAËLLE PETIT-PIERRE
RICHARD KORITZ

PHOTOGRAPHS BY:
HYMAN GOLDIN
HOWARD MENDELSOHN
NAN GOLDIN
RAYMOND COUVREU
JOHN JENKINSON
JOHN MARCHANT

DEDICATED TO ALL OUR SISTERS WHO HAVE DIED BY
SUICIDE OR HAVE BEEN INSTITUTIONALIZED FOR THEIR REBELLION

SISTERS, SAINTS AND SIBYLS
NAN GOLDIN

ACKNOWLEDGEMENTS

Work presented in 2026 by the Grand Palais at the Chapelle Saint-Louis de la Salpêtrière on the occassion of the retrospective exhibition *This Will Not End Well*.

Work presented by the Festival d'Automne in Paris from 16 September to 19 November 2004 at the Chapelle Saint-Louis de la Salpêtrière.

Commissioned by the Ministry of Culture and Communication, Delegation for Visual Arts and the National Centre for the Plastic Arts, and by the Festival d'Automne in Paris.
Production of film sequences: INA
With the support of Sylvie Winckler, Guy de Wouters, the Matthew Marks Gallery - New York, Michael Zilkha, Madame la Baronne Lambert, Maja Hoffman and Niccolo Spolverini, Jean-Claude Meyer.

Written and directed by Nan Goldin With Raymonde Couvreu
Scenography: Raymonde Couvreu
Photographs: Nan Goldin
Video: Raymonde Couvreu
Chief Editor and Producer: Nan Goldin
Production USA: John Marchant
Production Europe and technical production: Gwénaëlle Petit-Pierre

Additional video: John Marchant and John Jenkinson
Lighting: Marie-Christine Soma
Technical direction: Salahdine Khaitir
Construction: La Manufacture, Alain Merlaud
Alpinists: Verti Services

Stage Manager: Thierry Guyot
Lighting Manager: Raphael de Rosa
Stage Manager: Claude Cuisin
Electrician: Nathalie Desforges
Machinists: Sylvain Brizay and Clement de Renty

Thanks to Sylvie Blum (INA), Arte, the Chapelle, the Association of Friends of the Chapelle Saint-Louis de la Salpêtrière.

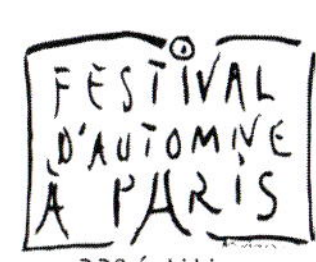
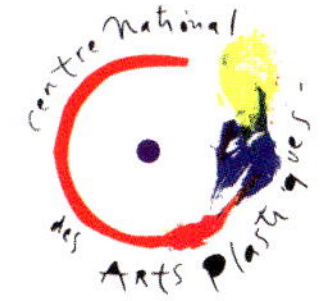
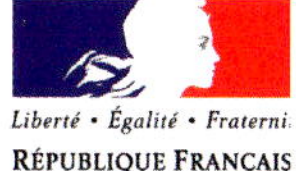
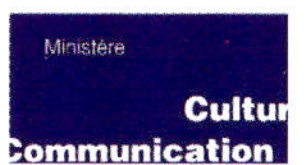

First published in 2004 by Éditions du Regard in collaboration with Le Festival d'Automne, Paris.

This edition published in the United Kingdom in 2026 by Thames & Hudson Ltd, 6-24 Britannia Street, London, WC1X 9JD

and in the United States of America in 2026 by Thames & Hudson Inc., 500 Fifth Avenue, New York, New York, 10110

Sisters, Saints and Sibyls © 2026 Thames & Hudson Ltd, London

Text © 2004 Nan Goldin
Photographs © Nan Goldin

Art direction and layout: Barbara Krkus
French translation of the bilingual edition: Denise Luccioni

EU Authorized Representative: Interart S.A.R.L.
19 rue Charles Auray, 93500 Pantin, Paris, France
PRODUCTSAFETY@THAMESHUDSON.CO.UK
INTERART.FR

A CIP catalogue record for this book is available from the British Library

ISBN 978-0-500-03104-9

01

Printed and bound in Italy by Printer Trento SrL

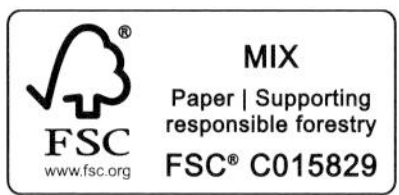

Be the first to know about our new releases,
exclusive content and author events by visiting

thamesandhudson.com
thamesandhudsonusa.com
thamesandhudson.com.au